The Book of Ganesha

The Book of
Ganesha

ROYINA GREWAL

PENGUIN BOOKS

PENGUIN BOOKS
Published by the Penguin Group
Penguin Books India Pvt. Ltd, 11 Community Centre, Panchsheel Park,
New Delhi 110 017, India
Penguin Group (USA) Inc., 375 Hudson Street, New York, New York
10014, USA
Penguin Group (Canada), 90 Eglinton Avenue East, Suite 700, Toronto,
Ontario, M4P 2Y3, Canada (a division of Pearson Penguin Canada Inc.)
Penguin Books Ltd, 80 Strand, London WC2R 0RL, England
Penguin Ireland, 25 St Stephen's Green, Dublin 2, Ireland (a division of Penguin
Books Ltd)
Penguin Group (Australia), 250 Camberwell Road, Camberwell, Victoria
3124, Australia (a division of Pearson Australia Group Pty Ltd)
Penguin Group (NZ), 67 Apollo Drive, Rosedale, Auckland 0632,
New Zealand (a division of Pearson New Zealand Ltd)
Penguin Group (South Africa) (Pty) Ltd, 24 Sturdee Avenue, Rosebank,
Johannesburg 2196, South Africa

Penguin Books Ltd, Registered Offices: 80 Strand, London WC2R 0RL,
England

First published in Viking by Penguin Books India 2001
Published in Penguin Books 2009

Text copyright © Royina Grewal 2001
Illustrations copyright © Penguin Books India 2001
Illustrations by Arvinder Chawla

All rights reserved

10 9 8 7 6 5 4

ISBN 9780143067603

Typeset in Sabon by Mantra Virtual Services, New Delhi
Printed at Anubha Printers, Noida

Contents

Varkratunda mahakaya surya koti sama prabha
Nirvighnam kuru mein deva sarva karyeshu sarvada

O Lord, with a twisted trunk and immense body,
Radiant with the effulgence of a million suns:
O Lord, may all our endeavours
Always be accomplished without obstacles.

Introduction

Shree Ganeshaaya Namaha
(Salutations to you, O Ganesha)

All Hindu prayers, all new endeavours, all the simple routines of daily life and especially all new books are preceded by this invocation.

Since Ganesha is very specially the patron deity of writers and since all books, particularly this one that attempts to grasp some nuances of his elusive essence, exist in his mind, the invocation to the elephant-headed god used by the Chalukya king Someshvara Malla at the beginning of his work *Manasollasa* is appropriate:

> *I prostrate myself before you, O Ganeshvara,*
> *Your icon is a hallowed charm*
> *That assures fulfilment of all desire.*
> *With the fanning of your broad ears,*
> *You scatter away all obstacles,*
> *As though they were weightless as cotton.*

To call upon Ganesha at the beginning of a new book is particularly important, for as Ganesha made it possible for sage Vyasa to complete the *Mahabharata*, so too did he impede the sage's compilation of the Puranas when he was not invoked.

Ganesha is one of the most widely worshipped deities in India, regarded by millions with love and adoration. Simple everyday routines, a new business, a journey, even an examination—all are preceded by a prayer to Ganesha, beseeching his benediction. Even little children in some parts of the country begin their writing lessons with the invocation *Harih Sri Ganapataya namaha* (Salutations to Ganesha, son of Shiva).

The elephant-headed deity transcends the boundaries of sect and caste, even of religion and geography. He is worshipped in many distant countries, invoked by Buddhists, Jains and all Hindus, high as well as low caste. Indeed, the emphatically non-sectarian temper of Ganesha worship inspired freedom fighter Bal Gangadhar Tilak to use Ganesha as an icon of concord. In the late nineteenth century, he initiated a community festival of Ganesha in Maharashtra, deliberately designed to bring people of various castes together and to forge a new unity in the freedom movement.

Ganesha is many things to many people. He is the portly, merry and mischievous childlike god, as well as the abstract philosopher. To his devotees he is the creator of the universe (a role more generally ascribed to Brahma) and also Siddhidata, the one who bestows blessings. He is the lord of obstacles, who removes impediments, but also creates all manner of difficulties if not propitiated. He is the presiding deity of material riches, and also the lord of spirituality. He is the guardian of the threshold who combats evil influences. To some he is also their primary personal god, their ishtadevta. Above all, Ganesha, more than any other deity, satisfies human aspirations for worldly success and fulfilment.

Ganesha is also a most accommodating deity, easy to please. He does not demand lengthy penance or austerities of his devotees but is contented by simple devotion, provided only that it is sincere.

The elephant-headed deity is one of the most frequently encountered icons of the Hindu pantheon. Images of Ganesha are often installed over the entrances to homes, shops, restaurants, office buildings—indeed almost any structure where people live or work—and many a framed picture presides over their interiors. He is present in every family shrine, where he is usually placed to the south, the direction of the demons, to defend the other gods from their baneful influences. He also wards off evil from the intersections of roads and the boundaries of villages, where he is often simply represented, like Shiva, as a rough stone daubed with red paint.

Icons are sculpted in most temples—at the threshold, in niches, in shrines, or in temple friezes associated with the mythology of Shiva. And today a living craft tradition revolves around the fashioning of clay images of the god, sold in the thousands during celebrations of Ganesha Chaturthi.

And yet, very few Hindus regard Ganesha as the primary deity of their devotion, possibly because he is one of the most recent deities to be incorporated into the Brahminical pantheon. Ganesha makes his appearance surprisingly late, only around the fifth century AD, when the imperial Gupta period was at its height and the early Puranas were being written. Although the name Gana-eshvara or Gana-sena does appear much earlier in the Vedas, scholars believe these references allude to Rudra Shiva or to Brihaspati, guru of the gods. And early images of an elephant-headed deity, including those on an Indo-Greek coin as well as sculptures from Mathura and elsewhere, dating between the first and third centuries BC, are believed to represent either an elephant demon or, at best, an early aspect of Ganesha as the demigod Vinayaka, the creator of obstacles.

Ganesha's rather abrupt entry into the mythology and iconography of Hinduism has resulted in a storm of controversy regarding his origins. The general

depredations

as Vinayaka

consensus holds that he originated from ancient animistic traditions as a pre-Aryan elephant deity. Jungle tribes propitiated this divinity to avert the depredations of the elephant herds that devastated fields and endangered life. Benefits from such worship were possibly later enlarged to encompass protection from all difficulties, a characteristic that ultimately came to be associated with the Ganesha of a later time.

But the transition was a long and slow process. Early writings describe the elephant-headed deity as Vighna-asura, the demon who creates obstacles. He was the leader of the malicious Vighnas who would cause endless problems for gods as well as humans if not regularly appeased. Although the chronology is somewhat murky, this demonic entity seems to have later evolved into the semi-divine but still ill-natured Vinayaka, son of Ambica, or Parvati, and the leader of Shiva's mischief-making attendants, the Ganas. He was an irascible deity, quick to take offence and thwart the performance of rituals, preventing devotees from reaping their benefits, if he was not paid sufficient attention. In this deity and his attributes are seen the origins of Ganesha Vinayaka, who hinders the falsely righteous and helps the truly devout.

early

absorbed

Ganesha is said to have acquired the ambivalent role of Vinayaka around the early fifth century. In the years that followed, the metamorphosis slowly came to completion. The demigod was absorbed into the Hindu pantheon as Shiva's son through the story of his beheading and symbolic rebirth with an elephant head. In several myths, Shiva repeatedly enunciates Ganesha's role as the lord of obstacles—but with a slight shift of emphasis from the earlier demonic aspects of Vinayaka to a benevolent manifestation—as he charges his son with the responsibility to maintain cosmic order. The negative role gradually gave way to the positive, and Ganesha, who was earlier beseeched not to cause problems, came to be worshipped to protect his devotees from all difficulties and evil.

The veneration of Ganesha received emphatic endorsement around the ninth century AD when the famous Samanta philosopher Shankaracharya popularized the panchayatana, the worship of the five major deities—Shiva, Vishnu, Surya, Devi and Ganesha, who are installed in household shrines and venerated on all auspicious occasions. Together they are considered to represent the five aspects of the one, the only God and to embody the five cosmic elements—water, air, fire, earth and ether. Ganesha

800's
↑

is the presiding deity of water, the aquatic element that, according to Hindu cosmology, preceded creation.

Around the tenth century, a religious order, the Ganapataya Sampradaya, gained momentum in Maharashtra. The Ganapatayas regarded Ganesha as the supreme being, the embodiment of transcendental reality, the all-pervading Brahman, creator of the cosmos, who bestows all gifts and removes all obstacles. The six sects within the Ganapatayas worshipped different forms of Ganesha with intense devotion, using varied mantras and yantras (or ritual diagrams). But they all looked upon the deity as the cause of creation, through whose maya the other gods appeared.

The Ganapatayas address Ganesha in prayers such as this:

> *Praise be to thee Ganesha,*
> *Thou art the visible Reality.*
> *Thou art the Creator, the Preserver, the*
>   *Destroyer.*
> *Thou art the Supreme Brahman, the Spirit*
>   *Manifest.*
> *The universe is born from Thee . . .*
> *Thou art Brahma, thou art Vishnu, thou*
>   *art Rudra Shiva.*

Thou art superior to the Trimurti.
Om. Praise be to thee, Ganesha

The devotions of the famous saint Moraya
Gòsavi, who lived at Morav near Pune in the late
sixteenth and early seventeenth centuries,
transformed the Ganapatayas into a powerful
religious movement. It is his son Chintamani,
however, who is the most famous devotee of the
lord and is credited with having built the Ganesha
temples at Moraya, Theur and Ranjangaon.

The extreme veneration of Ganesha in
Maharashtra gained a further dimension from his
status as the family deity of the powerful Peshwas,
the legendary prime ministers of the Maratha empire.
The famous Ganapati temple of Kasbapeth in Pune,
which is required to be visited before any auspicious
occasion, is believed to have been built by Shivaji's
mother around 1636. The devotion of the Peshwas
and their munificent grants contributed significantly
towards making Ganesha an important deity of the
Hindu pantheon.

Other individuals also played a great role in
enhancing the popularity of Ganesha. The poet
Ramadasa (1608-82) addressed Ganesha frequently

in his compositions. One of the most common songs of benediction, sung as the finale of Ganesha worship in Maharashtra, was composed by Ramadasa. It begins by describing Ganesha as the harbinger of happiness and the one who dispels distress.

The sacred literature of Ganesha proliferated under the patronage of the Ganapatayas. A new Upanishad was developed, as well as various Puranas. The mythology of Ganesha is the special focus of the Ganesha Upapurana, the 'Ganapati khanda' of the Brahmavaivarta Purana, the Ganesha Gita and the Vinayaka Mahatmaya. Passionate hymns and eulogies were composed in honour of Ganesha, each crafted with enormous skill and leavened with devotion. Couched in complicated metres and elaborate figures of speech or alamkaras, many of these are among the poetic masterpieces of the Indian tradition.

But Ganesha is not solely a deity of the subcontinent. Early evidence of the presence of elephant-headed deities extend from Afghanistan through Central Asia, Tibet and Mongolia to China and Japan, and from Burma to Thailand, Laos, Cambodia, Vietnam, Indonesia and Borneo in the Pacific. There is evidence of an elephant-headed god even in distant Mexico.

in early
Aryan

Figures of deities that are half-elephant and half-man, dating to the early Aryan period, have been excavated from the trans-Oxonian region and are believed to reflect the extreme veneration accorded to elephants. Elephant-headed deities are particularly

in B'ism

prominent in the Buddhist pantheons of Tibet, China and Japan, and many of these are believed to be derived from ancient Indian tantric traditions. Tantric practices were an important component of Ganapataya rites and also influenced representations of Ganesha. Thirty texts in the sacred literature of Tibet, said to be translations from Indian originals, dwell on Ganesha in his tantric aspect. Although Ganesha's relationship with Shiva is acknowledged in some of these writings, he is largely identified as an incarnation of the compassionate Bodhisattva Avalokiteshwara, foremost among the enlightened ones in the Buddhist pantheon. Ritual practices dedicated to Ganesha as a Buddhist tantric deity, from whom food, wealth, sex and supernatural powers may be acquired, survive to this day.

In China, the elephant-headed deity, Vinayaka, the obstructer, was regarded largely as a negative force who must be subdued through potent rituals and the chanting of special mantras. This perspective seems to have developed from ancient

Chinese myths that associated elephant-headed CHINA
creatures with evil. The Japanese Shingon school of JAPAN
Buddhism, however, developed a popular and still
current cult around two elephant-headed figures—
one male and one female—standing in embrace.
Worship of this deity, still immensely popular, is
specifically directed towards the attainment of
material and sexual goals.

In South-East Asia, Ganesha is often largely a SEA
Hindu deity, widely invoked to remove obstacles.
In Thailand as well as the islands of Indonesia, there
are images of Ganesha in friezes associated with
the mythology of Shiva. Besides these, some very
large images of Ganesha have also been found that
seem to have been installed in temples dedicated to
the deity. Such icons have led scholars to believe SEA
that Ganesha was the focus of a cult as an ishtadevta,
a primary personal deity, perhaps earlier than in
India.

Ganesha's multifaceted persona descends to MYTHS
mankind through a multitude of myths. These span
the entire gamut of his manifestations, from his
distinction as a supreme being to his somewhat
diminished status as a subsidiary deity. Whatever
his stature, these intricate narratives contained in
the Puranas—especially in the forty-six chapters of

the Ganapati khanda of the Brahmavaivarta Purana—as well as the Upapuranas, are told with love, verve and great empathy.

Such is the urgency of man's quest to penetrate the realms of mystery and miracle, such is his need for the continued presence of divine revelation that myths continue to evolve even in the present. A few years ago it was said that images of Ganesha were drinking milk all over the world, and this was understood as a sign of benediction to the devout. The belief that Santoshi Ma, the benign mother who grants devotees health, happiness and successful marriages, is Ganesha's daughter is also relatively new. Such modern myths have been absorbed into the huge body of sacred lore that continues to inspire wonderment and sustain boundless devotion.

The myths and stories about Ganesha retold in this book are only a few of the great number that exist in sacred texts and folklore. As with all myths, these too were handed down orally, embellished by generation after generation with humour, exaggeration and often pure fantasy, as mortals tried to grasp the divine. Some also have a historical perspective and often contain reflections of cultural conquests and fusions, as one race became enriched by the inherited wisdom and images of another. But they do not follow any coherent chronology, nor are they consistent. Insights are combined and recombined in reckless disregard of sequence. There is no standard list of facts, no common conclusion, only a deepened sense of possibility. The myths are the product of a different way of knowing which combines an untrammelled imagination with human hopes and dreams.

The composers of myths were not bound by the constraints of linear time. They treated time as cyclic and fluid, in which past, present and future are interconnected in a reality larger than our aspirations, richer and more complex than our dreams. Whether the myths are historically 'true' or not is irrelevant. What is important is the message they convey, the allegory they represent, the philosophical and moral messages they are structured to reveal.

Listen then to these stories with your inner self. Suspend reality and judgement, suspend conventional time frames and parameters, absorb the subtle and indirect messages, open the doors to another world where Ganesha is, always was and will be in all eternity.

Origins

Origins

Om. Obeisance to you, Ganapati.
Only you are the visible reality.
Only you alone are the creator.
Only you alone are the preserver.
Only you alone are the destroyer.

—Ganesha Athavashirsha Upanishad

The universe was still and silent, enveloped in darkness. Suddenly a booming sound came into being. It grew in volume and intensity till it penetrated every corner of the cosmos with the divine reverberation: Om . . . Om . . . Om.

A shimmering radiance suffused the sky, illumining the figure of Ganesha that emanated from the Supreme Brahman. He had become manifest to recreate the universe after it had been destroyed by the burning heat of twelve suns.

Ganesha whirled in the blinding light in the cosmic dance of creation. His feet moved so fast that he was in a thousand places at once. As his dance drew to an end, Ganesha raised his conch and blew it. Once again the sound of creation, Om, resonated through the universe.

He then summoned the three great gods, Brahma, Vishnu and Shiva, and assigned them the duties of creation, preservation and destruction. 'Go forth,' he instructed them, 'and nurture the world.'

Ganesha further said, 'I am the Universe. Inside me is all that was, is and will be. Enter me and seek Truth and Knowledge.' Saying this, he lifted the great gods and swallowed them. The gods found themselves in a colourful world inside Ganesha. It seemed as though they were looking into millions of mirrors, each reflecting a thousand images. They saw themselves as they had been, as they were and as they would be. They saw fourteen different worlds. They saw the gods and the demons, the gandharvas and the apsaras, the musicians and the dancers of the heavens. They saw the sages doing penance. And they understood what had to be done.

Brahma set about the work of creation. But several impediments soon arose. The beings he created took on strange forms. Ganesha reappeared and rebuked Brahma, 'You are in difficulty because you did not think of me while you were creating the world.' Chastened, Brahma realized that his arrogance and self-absorption had made him incapable of creation. He appealed to Ganesha to give him the energy to complete his task. Ganesha told Brahma to pray to the two attributes within him of siddhi and buddhi, spiritual attainment and wisdom, and with their help the world came into being.

This story from the Ganesha Upanishad of the Ganapataya tradition marks the culmination of the elephant-headed deity's absorption into the Hindu pantheon and establishes, without question, his overweening supremacy over even the great gods of Hinduism. Although this particular myth endows Ganesha with pre-eminence as the manifestation of the Supreme Brahman, the causative factor of creation, scores of other popular myths mark the several stages in the deity's long journey to this exalted position.

Many of these dwell upon Ganesha's origin, but with multiple variations and often confusing contradictions. The inconsistencies in the different

stories are easily explained. They tell of diverse
episodes that relate to different incarnations of
Ganesha after each of the many dissolutions of the
universe and to his many manifestations to combat
evil demons.

In most myths, Ganesha is introduced as the
son of Parvati. Only in very exceptional cases is it
Shiva who creates Ganesha. But the divine couple
never come together to beget Ganesha. For, like
many other important deities of the Hindu pantheon,
Ganesha is not conceived in the normal sense. He is
too potent a deity to be born of the union of even a
god and a goddess. One story explains why he cannot
be begotten by Shiva and Parvati.

Once Shiva and Parvati were making love.
Such was the power generated by their union
that the three worlds shuddered and great
waves swept the seven oceans. All creatures
trembled with terror. The gods realized that
a child born of such passion would also be
endowed with the combined energies of
Shiva and Parvati. Such a being would
overshadow even their own considerable
powers and would be especially invincible.

Various stratagems were devised over the cosmic epochs to prevent such a dreadful occurrence. On one occasion the gods convinced Shiva to have no children. Parvati was furious and cursed the wives of other gods that they too would remain barren. Therefore it is said that the children of the gods are 'mind born' or begotten in some mysterious manner. (An ingenuous story, which enabled goddesses to retain the special status and power associated in most religious systems with virginity.)

Even when the gods prevailed upon Shiva to beget Kartika, they persuaded him to have his semen drunk by Agni rather than allow it to enter Parvati's womb. Another myth with strong Vaishnava overtones describes how even Vishnu intervened to prevent Parvati from conceiving.

> Shiva and Parvati had been in seclusion for a thousand years. The gods became fearful of the consequences and sought Vishnu's help. He disguised himself as a beggar and disturbed the divine couple in their lovemaking. Just in time. For in their haste to cover themselves, Shiva's semen spilt on the bed. The beggar vanished and a newborn boy child appeared in his place. This was Ganesha.

A few myths find a compromise and explain that Ganesha was created by the union of the sexual essences of Shiva and Parvati, but outside their bodies. Sometimes it is the mingling of their sweat, a symbol of sexual fluids, that gives rise to Ganesha, at other times a drop of blood shed during intercourse.

Other solutions to the impediment of their bearing a child together present Shiva and Parvati taking on the form of elephants to create their elephant-headed son.

> One day when Shiva and Parvati were in the audience hall of the gods, an inscription of the sacred syllable Om caught their attention. Parvati was particularly inspired by its resemblance to the profile of an elephant. She told her divine husband that she desired that they both take the form of elephants, which they did, and of their coupling was born the elephant-headed Ganesha.

That is why, say his devotees, Ganesha is also called Omkara. Since the sacred syllable is the sound that preceded creation, Ganesha is worshipped at the beginning of all ritual.

A myth from South India tells of another
occasion when Shiva and Parvati come together as
elephants to beget their elephant-headed son.

> Ganesha asks his father how it was that he
> had an elephant's head while his parents
> did not. Shiva explains that once when he
> and Parvati had retired to the verdant valleys
> of the Himalayas to be with each other,
> they watched elephants mating. This
> inspired them to become elephants and to
> enjoy themselves in a similar manner. And
> out of their passion Ganesha was born.

When Shiva himself creates Ganesha, he does
so asexually, without the participation of Parvati.
As son of Shiva, Ganesha is called Shivaputra,
Shambhutanya and Shambhusuta.

> In the days when piety prevailed, the gods
> and sages who practised austerities reaped
> rich rewards. But later the forces of evil,
> the asuras and the rakshasas, performed
> sacrifices and rituals through which they
> received boons from Shiva. Emboldened,
> they began to attack and defeat the gods,

and gained dominance. Indra and other gods complained to Shiva and implored him to create a being who would throw obstacles in the way of those who used divine rewards for improper ends. They asked Shiva to subvert the attempts of the asuras and rakshasas to perform pious acts and thus make it impossible for them to receive any more protective boons.

As the gods spoke, Shiva looked at Uma with desire and laughed joyously. A glorious youth emanated from his mouth. He looked exactly like Shiva and was endowed with all the same qualities.

Brahma told the gods that Shiva had created this beauteous youth to create obstacles for evil. He would be the leader of the Vinayakas, who created impediments.

While the gods thanked Shiva for answering their prayers, Uma looked upon the exquisite young man with unconscious desire. Shiva perceived her fickleness, which, according to this story, 'is the natural condition of women'. He became angry that the beauty of his creation had caused even his chaste wife Uma to falter. So the lord cursed

Ganesha, 'Thou shalt have an elephant's head,' he said with anger, 'and a pot belly; a garland of serpents shall be thy adornment.'

Shiva went on to enunciate the names of his son—Ganesha, Vinayaka and Vighnaraja. 'Success and disappointment shall proceed from thee,' Shiva proclaimed, 'and thou shalt place impediments to prevent the forces of evil from performing virtuous acts but will render all assistance to the devas and other good beings in their endeavour to perform such rites.'

From this it is clear that Vinayaka received from Shiva the dual duties of hindering as well as facilitating acts of virtue according to the motives with which they were initiated.

More often, however, Ganesha is clearly Parvati's child. The myths repeatedly present the goddess, who is anxious to have a son, attempting to convince Shiva to father her child. Shiva, however, insists that he neither needs nor wants a son. Sons, he tells his wife, are desired by ordinary men who require them to perform the rites of death. 'I am not subject to death, so I do not need a son.'

'O Devi,' he says, 'when there is no illness, what is the use of taking medicine against it?'

But Parvati's desire for a child is overwhelming. 'I yearn painfully for the kiss of a son,' she tells Shiva and reminds him of his duties as a husband. 'Since you took me for your wife you should give me a son.' Her maternal instincts are so strong that she poignantly absolves Shiva of all paternal responsibility. 'When you have given me a child, you can return to your yoga, great lord. I will bring up the son and you can be a yogi.' She goes even further and promises that if necessary, their son will not desire marriage so that her husband will not be burdened with descendants. But Shiva remains adamant.

According to one myth, though, Shiva does give in.

Besieged by Parvati's repeated pleas for a son, he finally promises to make one for her. He takes her clothes and shapes them into the form of a child. Parvati is delighted and cradles the doll on her lap. She playfully puts it to her breast and the doll comes to life as Ganesha and calls her 'Ma'.

In another version, the doll becomes alive when it falls to the ground. In this and other myths, Ganesha does not yet have an elephant head. He gets it later when he is reborn with new responsibilities. Even in the myth of Shiva's creation of Ganesha, he is a most handsome youth who receives his elephant head only when his father condemns him to lose his beauty. Ganesha's inception as a doll is presented in another story with a slightly different slant.

> During one of Shiva's lengthy absences, Parvati became dispirited and thought of creating a son to ease her loneliness. She played with her friends at making dolls from the unguents of her body and formed a male doll with the head of an elephant. This she playfully threw into the Ganga, whereupon the doll came to life as Ganesha. His body expanded enormously, until he filled the entire world. Parvati called him son, but so did Ganga. This is the reason why Ganesha is also called Gangeya.

Here the power of the river goddess Ganga is emphasized. She is the nurturing mother who gives life to Ganesha, bringing the added dimensions of her sanctity to him. This myth also recalls other stories about the legendary conflict between Parvati and Ganga over Shiva's affections and resolves the antagonism between them that had simmered through the ages.

The unguents of Parvati's body are a particularly appropriate medium for the creation of her son since the bath water of deities is considered to be as sacred and life giving as the urine and dung of holy cows. The use of unguents in forming Ganesha is fundamental to many myths.

Just as Shiva is said to have created Ganesha to place obstacles for the falsely righteous, so too did Parvati bring her son into being for the same purpose.

> During the twilight that intervened between the Dwapara yuga and the Kali yuga, Shiva had granted a boon that guaranteed salvation to all who worshipped at the temple dedicated to him at Somnath, irrespective of their misdeeds, caste or even gender.
> Thus women, barbarians who were ignorant of the holy scriptures, shudras and

other sinners, all gained entrance to heaven
just by worshipping at Somnath. With such
an easy course available, people ceased to
perform penance, sacrifices and other pious
acts. Heaven became so overcrowded that
even the gods had to stand with their hands
straight up. Yama, the lord of dharma, was
discomfited when he realized that despite
the evil deeds of men, the seven hells were
empty. The gods appealed to Shiva, but he
was helpless for he had granted the
unconditional boon to devotees who
venerated him at Somnath. Parvati came
to their rescue. She created Ganesha from
the scented unguents of her body and said
to the gods, 'For your sake I have brought
forth this being to place hindrances before
men so that they will become filled with
great delusion, their wits defeated by desire,
and they will not come to Somnath.'
Parvati explained Ganesha's responsibility
to him and emphasized, 'But for those that
propitiate thee by the following hymn do
thou remove all obstacles and enable them
to obtain the favour of Shiva and worship
at Somnath.'

Om, I praise thee, O lord of Difficulties!
Beloved spouse of Siddhi and Buddhi,
                                Ganapati,
Who places obstacles before men who do
                        not worship thee,
I praise thee O Ganesha!
Dreadful son of Uma, but firm and easily
                            propitiated!
O Vinayaka I praise thee!
O Elephant-faced One,
Who didst formerly protect the gods and
                    accomplish their wishes,
I praise thee!

'And so,' said Parvati, 'shalt thou be praised
and worshipped on the fourth of each half
month.'

Thus is Ganesha entrusted with maintaining the
rule of righteousness. The myth also establishes his
dual role as the one who both removes and places
obstacles. Moreover, the success he bestows upon
human undertakings is understood to be in response
to the homage of devotees. Ganesha's ambivalence
is also a partial reflection of the characteristics of
his divine parents, in both of whom intensely

destructive and terrifying aspects are juxtaposed with
extreme benevolence and compassion. It is natural,
therefore, that their son should share their terrible
as well as beneficent manifestations.

Other myths of Ganesha's creation by Parvati
encompass his birth, beheading and rebirth. In the
most popular version, Ganesha is born with a
human head, later substituted with that of an
elephant.

Although Shiva and Parvati were married,
Shiva was less than an ideal husband. An
ascetic who cared little for worldly
pleasures, he often retired to spend years in
meditation. Among Parvati's favourite
diversions during his lengthy absences was
to linger at her bath with her companions
Jaya and Vijaya. Once as they were
splashing about playfully, Shiva appeared
unexpectedly, greatly embarrassing the
dishevelled ladies.

All too soon the time came for him to
depart. Parvati was bereft and became
increasingly lonely. One day while bathing
languorously in her pool, she decided to
create a son who would divert her and also

shower her with the love and protection she craved. She gathered the perfumed unguents that she had rubbed into her body and formed from them the most beautiful of sons, whom she imbued with life.

The boy grew in beauty and strength. Recalling her divine husband's unseemly intrusion when she and her companions were bathing, Parvati gave her son a mace, with instructions to henceforth prevent anyone from entering the bath chamber without her permission. Several years passed. The boy performed his duty well and Parvati and her ladies bathed without fear of interruption.

One day Shiva returned from his meditation without prior warning. When he made to enter his wife's bath chamber, he was accosted by this unknown boy. Neither knew the other. The son asked the husband to wait while he obtained his mother's permission. Shiva's chief attendant, Nandi, attempted to persuade the boy to allow his lord to enter. The boy remained adamant. Persuasion gave way to threat. Heated words were exchanged in loud voices.

Parvati lingered in her bath, till violent
noises outside her chamber indicated that a
furious fight was in progress. She rushed to
the door to find her son decapitated by her
furious husband.

Parvati was overcome with grief and anger.
Her distress moved her husband and her
threats to bring the universe to destruction
initiated urgent remedies.

Shiva dispatched his attendants to the north,
the auspicious direction, and instructed them
to bring back the head of the first being
they encountered. This, of course, was an
elephant. When the elephant head was
affixed on the beheaded boy and he was
brought back to life, Shiva declared he
would henceforth be the leader of his
attendants, the ganas. Hence the name
Gana-esha, lord of Shiva's troops.

Ganesha is thus created, destroyed and reborn
to a higher status. Death becomes a bridge to greater
things. The episode reinforces the Hindu cyclic
concept of the universe that repeatedly disintegrates
and is recreated.

Many aspects of this myth are said to parallel

the Hindu thread ceremony, where a young man is symbolically reborn into the upper castes, the twice born. The ceremony involves a simulation of death and rebirth process.

An allegorical message is also contained in the beheading of Parvati's son. When the ego is too assertive, Shiva cuts it off, destroying darkness and ignorance. So too does Ganesha aid his devotees to rise beyond the limitations of self, helping them to be reborn into eternity. The decapitation, then, signifies Ganesha's elevation to heightened consciousness and his transformation into a superior deity.

Ganesha's conflict with Shiva is believed to symbolize Aryan victory over a tribe with an elephant totem. The beheading, to cleanse and remove all polluting influences, and the subsequent 'rebirth' as son of Shiva, is also said to represent the process whereby the folk deity was absorbed into mainstream Hinduism. Ganesha's restoration with even greater power is in keeping with the pragmatic Aryan understanding that ancient folk deities should not be crushed but assimilated and given places of honour among their gods.

After Ganesha was reborn with his elephant head, Shiva took part in the rites appropriate to the birth of a son. He held Ganesha in his arms, kissed him on the head and said, 'You are my son who has been born to destroy the demons and aid the gods as well as the Brahmins who teach the Vedas. Stand astride the path which leads to heaven and create obstacles in the rites of anyone who has performed sacrifices but not paid the priest's fee.' Shiva also declared that henceforth Ganesha would be addressed at the beginning of any ritual in heaven or earth.

Shiva thus delegated powers and status to his wife's son, endorsing his transition from a local deity to a powerful member of the Hindu pantheon. He makes it clear, in this and other myths, that he approves of Parvati's child and is happy to accept him as his son by legitimizing Ganesha's birth and enhancing his stature. But Shiva emphasizes that Ganesha was not sired by him. In one myth he explains that Ganesha will be called Vinayaka because he was born nayakena vina, without the intervention of a husband.

Such was the popularity of the elephant-headed deity that Vaishnavas also wished to claim him as their own and developed myths to establish the connection of Ganesha with Vishnu. One presents Ganesha as an incarnation of Krishna, with Shani instead of Shiva as the agent of beheading. And it is Vishnu who revives Ganesha and grants him his special status.

Shiva advised Parvati, who wanted to have a son, to propitiate Vishnu and observe vratas (fasts and rituals) in his honour for a year. 'Then,' he said, 'the lord of gopikas, Krishna himself, will be born as your son.' Parvati observed the vrata, and to her immense joy, Krishna was born to her as an infant of unparalleled beauty.

All the gods came to pay homage to Parvati's new son. The great ascetic Shani, son of Surya, was among them, but he kept his eyes cast down and would not look at the child. When Parvati asked him the reason for this, he explained that once he had been so absorbed in the contemplation of lord Vishnu that he had not noticed his wife's attempts to gain his attention. Furious that her fertile time would pass unfulfilled, she had cursed him, saying that anything his eyes rested upon would be destroyed. It was because of this that he would not look at the child.

Parvati and her attendants mocked Shani and she demanded that he admire her son. And so with great fear, and only out of the corner of his eye, Shani looked at Parvati's infant and his glance instantly severed the child's head. Vishnu, moved by the mother's grief, flew off on Garuda towards the north. He brought back the head of a young elephant which he joined to the headless body of Parvati's son, reviving him. Vishnu blessed 'Krishna'-Ganesha thus:

May your puja be performed before that of
any other God.
May you be situated in all venerable beings
and may you be the best among yogis.
This is my boon to you.

This is a perfect example of the manner in which myths were constantly recast in keeping with the varying imperatives of the time. They dissolve into newer, fresher, more relevant transformations in an exciting, dynamic process that is a continuous celebration of life and its mysteries. Myths such as this one that associate Vishnu, Krishna and Shani with the mythology of Ganesha develop a great connecting pattern that invests the deity with several supplementary dimensions. This process of extension is furthered in other versions which identify the elephant that was beheaded so that Ganesha may be reborn. Thus the deity is linked to other mythological elephants, whose noble qualities, described in the myths, are then assigned to Ganesha.

> When Vishnu flew off on Garuda he entered a dense forest. There he came across Gajendra, the king of elephants, sleeping, surrounded by his wives and calves. As Vishnu cut off the beautiful head of Gajendra, his mate awoke and, with her children, began to lament. Vishnu consoled the grieving elephants. He cut off the head of another elephant, attached it Gajendra's body and restored him to life. And then he took Gajendra's head back and joined it to Ganesha's body.

Even though Gajendra is restored to life, his legendary majesty, benevolence and compassion are brought to bear on Ganesha in an intricate web of kinship.

In another myth, it is the demon elephant Gajasura whom Shiva kills and decapitates to restore Parvati's son.

The demon Gajasura was a great devotee of Shiva. He prayed and practised austerities in the name of the great god for many years. Shiva was pleased with his devotion and promised to grant Gajasura a wish. The demon made the astonishing request that he wanted Shiva in his stomach. The god complied. Parvati was devastated and sought the aid of Vishnu, who conceived an elaborate plan. He disguised himself as a musician, persuaded Brahma to be his tabla player and Nandi their dancing bull. Together they performed before Gajasura. Nandi danced so beautifully that the elephant demon was enchanted and asked what he could give the troupe in reward. 'Give us back our Shiva,' they begged.

Gajasura agreed, even though he realized
that once Shiva was removed from his
stomach he would die. So he beseeched the
god to take his life but make his elephant's
head, his gajamukha, so important that
everyone would worship it.

Although this recalls the early demonic
associations of Ganesha, the demon here appears in
a more positive aspect.

According to another myth, Shiva's attendant
Nandi beheaded Indra's divine white elephant,
Airavata, one of the celestial creatures retrieved
during the churning of the ocean.

Nandi wandered the triple universe to find
a suitable head for Parvati's decapitated
son. Eventually, he came across Airavata
lying down with his head towards the north.
As Nandi prepared to behead this
magnificent beast, the elephant trumpeted
loudly in fear. Indra came to the rescue of
his mount and fought fiercely in his defence.
But he was defeated and Nandi made off
with Airavata's noble head.

As the mount of Indra, king of the gods and lord of rain, Airavata brings to Ganesha the majesty and dignity of a royal elephant. Airavata also frequently carried Indra to battle and was most accomplished in combat, an ability shared by the deity who acquired his head. More importantly, Airavata, who originated in the cosmic ocean, was also charged with the responsibility of drawing up water from the underworld which Indra would rain down on earth. His head, therefore, invested Ganesha with connotations of fertility and prosperity associated with life-giving rain.

In some myths, however, Ganesha is actually created by Parvati with an elephant's head.

When Parvati formed her long-desired son from the fragrant essences and herbs she had rubbed into her body, she discovered that she did not have enough to complete the head. So she urgently called out to her other son Kartikeya for help. He rushed out, saw a superb elephant in rut, cut off its head and attached it to the body his mother had made, even as Parvati cried out, 'It's too large, don't, don't!'

In Thailand, Ganesha is viewed as the progenitor of elephants and is the focus of special veneration among elephant trainers. In more aristocratic circles, however, the myths evolved further. The royal tonsure ceremony in Thailand presented another version of the beheading. During this ceremony, the Thai king took on the role of Shiva while his son was seen as Ganesha. The ceremony itself took place on a specially built replica on Mount Kailasha. Myths that enlarge upon this association treat Ganesha as identical with Kartikeya.

Kartikeya Skanda, the son of Shiva, was due to set off on a journey. His father decided to have his head tonsured before his departure. All the gods were invited to bless the boy on this auspicious occasion. But during the ceremony, Vishnu made a thoughtless remark, which caused Kartikeya's head to fall off. An elephant's head was grafted on his body to restore him to life and he was renamed Maha Vighneshwara.

The often-confusing accretions and additions to the mythology of Ganesha are evidence of the simple and often outrageous explanations through which rustic populations found answers to puzzling aspects of the Ganesha story. Thus Kartikeya Skanda becomes identical with Ganesha.

The Buddhist version of the myth describes Shiva holding a lavish ceremonial to tonsure both his sons. All the gods were invited, except the Buddha. This omission caused the ceremonies to end in disaster. A fierce wind sprang up and whipped Shiva's sword from his hand, flinging it through the air to sever both the boys' heads. The boys were then brought back to life by attaching elephant heads to their bodies.

Ganesha's head also signifies the qualities he shares with elephants in general. Although many myths describe the processes by which Ganesha acquired his elephant head, none explain why his head was that of an elephant rather than of any other creature. One possible answer could be the sanctity attached to elephants in ancient India, expressed in the worship of elephants and elephant-headed deities. The sheer size of elephants inspired awe that was translated over the aeons to reverence and eventually to the elephant as a sacred symbol of strength, stability and protection.

Elephants were presented with other animals in a quasi-sacred context in the famous Pashupati seal of Harappa. Such was the significance of elephants that deities called Dantin (The Tusked One), Hastimukha (The Elephant-faced One) and Vakratunda (The One with a Twisted Trunk) seem to have had a popular following even in the Vedic period.

The worship of elephants became especially prevalent towards the end of the first millennium, when elephant deities were also revered by Greek generals and their satraps. Greek writers of the time describe a very old elephant at Taxila, said to have once belonged to Porus, which was venerated by the local people who anointed it with fragrant herbs and decorated it with jewels. In the north-west, hill features that resembled an elephant were often looked upon as the special deity of the region or as a protective divinity that looked after travellers.

To the Greeks, after Alexander, the elephant was a symbol of victory. Some kings were depicted with the head of an elephant, while others were represented with an elephant scalp in their headdress to signify might and bravery. Elephant motifs continued to be closely associated with royalty in succeeding generations.

Numerous Buddhist Jataka tales present the elephant as a most virtuous creature and celebrate its qualities of loyalty, wisdom, prudence and compassion. Indeed such was its sanctity and perceived nobility that the elephant is closely associated with the conception of the Buddha.

When the Bodhisattva decided to descend from the Tusita heaven to become incarnate as Gautama, he took on the form of a mystical white elephant and entered the womb of Queen Maya. Other versions present the queen dreaming of this occurrence.

Another story insists that in a previous birth the Bodhisattva was Saddanta, a six-tusked white elephant who as the king of elephants embodied the virtues of charity and compassion.

The Hastyayurveda, a text on the wisdom and longevity of elephants, warns that if elephants are not honoured, the king, his army and his kingdom will be doomed. But if due respect is paid to elephants, the country will prosper, Indra will send plentiful rain, crops will sprout in time, there will be no plague, no drought.

In art and literature, elephants were commonly identified with water. This relationship is expressed in the several depictions of goddess Lakshmi being bathed by water poured from golden vessels held in the trunks of celestial elephants. The aquatic symbolism was further amplified by poetic metaphors which compared the elephant to dark rain clouds, enhancing by implication Ganesha's eminence as the god of plenty and agricultural fertility.

The legendary funerals that elephants are said to conduct for their dead augmented their distinction, while their vegetarianism enhanced their reputed purity. Their size and majesty made them the most appropriate ceremonial vehicle for the highest temporal authority and the backbone of ancient armies.

The enormous strength of elephants, however, can also be directed towards destruction. They have long memories of deliberate injuries inflicted on them and can be vengeful, just as Ganesha is intolerant of wilful misdeeds. The familiar depredations of elephants, the fear they inspire in the wild, their fury when crossed, all make it easy to understand their association with obstacles. According to Rajput folklore, a king would gift an elephant to nobles who displeased him, confident that the cost of feeding an elephant would ruin them forever.

Because of their size and strength, elephants

were believed to hold the world on their shoulders and to guard its portals—a role visually expressed in the great temple complexes, where sculpted rows of elephants decorate and 'support' temple plinths while elephant statues guard temple thresholds. As indeed does Ganesha.

Another story elaborates.

Elephants are said to have been born from the cosmic egg, the hiranyagarbha, out of which the sun emerged. Brahma breathed life into the two halves of the broken egg. Airavata and eight male elephants came into being from one half and from the other were born eight female elephants who became their consorts. The Ashtadikpalas, the eight guardians of the directions, commandeered the magnificent creatures as their mounts and enlisted their aid to protect the world.

In some myths, these elephants are viewed as demonic forces that are destroyed by successive incarnations of Ganesha. The demons include Kamasura (lust), Krodhasura (anger), Lobhasura (greed), Mohasura (delusion), Maatsaryasura (envy),

Mamasura (ego), Abhimasura (pride) and Istasura
(self-absorption). Ganesha came to earth eight times
to battle these allegoric representations of vices, thus
helping his devotees overcome them. In each of his
incarnations, Ganesha is known by a different name.
For example, he is said to have become Gajanana,
elephant headed, to overcome the demons Lobhasura
and Mohasura.

> Kubera, the god of wealth and certainly the
> richest among the gods, meditated for many
> years to please Shiva and Parvati. Impressed
> by his devotion, the divine couple appeared
> before him. But Kubera's austerities had not
> brought him humility. So enamoured was
> he of his own wealth that he thought the
> goddess would be attracted to him for his
> riches. He cast amorous glances at Parvati
> and out of his evil thoughts sprung the
> demons Lobhasura and Mohasura. Parvati
> was furious at his impertinence and her
> anger gave rise to Gajanana, her elephant-
> headed son who destroyed the demons.

This story reminds devotees that it is essential
to subdue greed and delusions, otherwise Ganesha's

wrath will wreak havoc in their lives.

Ganesha became incarnate as Vakratunda, literally, the one with a twisted trunk, to subdue the demon of envy, Maatsaryasura.

> Now Indra, who according to this story, is also the lord of the mind, was a very careless god. He often wandered off in pursuit of various celestial damsels, heedless of his duties. On one such occasion, the mind was left untended and Maatsaryasura was born. The demon invaded the mind and caused previously unheard of feelings of jealousy, covetousness, spite, rivalry and malice to taint the minds of men. The impact of these blemishes soon spread in the world, bringing discord and friction. Vakratunda appeared, seized the demon from the mind with his curving trunk, destroyed him and restored harmony among men. To this day, he continues to do so, placing obstacles before those who are consumed by envy.

Vikata, the gigantic, was the form Ganesha took to overcome the demon of lust, Kamasura.

Kamasura was a great devotee of Vishnu and performed many pious acts in his honour, which gained him many boons. He married Trishna (Desire) and had two sons, decay and corruption. Together they wreaked havoc among gods and men. Since lust is insatiable, it cannot be resolved, only eradicated by annihilation. Kamasura was protected by his boons and could not be destroyed by gods or men. Ganesha took the colossal form of Vikata. He filled the earth and the sky and all the things with his presence. Kamasura and his sons were destroyed and the world was freed of lust and corruption. And to this day, Vikata continues to destroy those among whom these vices persist, restoring cosmic harmony.

The demon of ego, Mamasura, born from Parvati's laughter, was ensnared by delusion. He was obsessed with the self, which only Ganesha as Vighnaraja could destroy.

Lambodara, the pot-bellied, became manifest to overcome the demon of anger, Krodhasura.

When the cosmic ocean was churned and the asuras and devas quarrelled over the nectar of immortality that emerged, Vishnu took the form of Mohini and came together with Lord Shiva. Of this encounter was born the demon Krodhasura. Wrath ruled the world, causing indescribable anguish to men and gods. Now, as everyone knows, anger must be swallowed. So Ganesha became incarnate as Lambodara and took in Krodhasura in one huge gulp. Which is why Lambodara has a such a huge belly.

The name Lambodara is also said to have derived from Ganesha's proclivity for sweets and his immense hunger.

Besides these, Ganesha is known by many more names, some say at least a thousand. These describe different aspects of the deity, ranging from his physical characteristics to his qualities or attributes, and are often linked to his various manifestations. Although Ganesha is infinite in his incarnations, three primary forms are said to have become manifest at the beginning of each of the yugas or epochs of cosmic time.

In halcyon days of the Treta or golden age he

was golden-hued and ten-armed, mounted on a lion.
During the Dwaypa, associated with silver, Ganesha
appeared as white-coloured and six-armed, astride
a peacock. In the copper age, the Dwapara yuga,
the cosmic age prior to the present Kali yuga,
Ganesha defeated the red demon Sindura, whose
copious outpouring of blood turned the elephant-
headed deity red, daubed with the essence of Sindura.

A fourth manifestation is yet to come in this
present Kali yuga or iron age when he will return
black in colour and two-armed, astride a horse, to
destroy confusion, terrorism, negativity and all dark
powers. His name will be Dhumraketu.

Despite his many names and forms, however,
Ganesha is regarded above all as an aspect of the
one, the only God. Each of his manifestations is
said to represent a particular aspect of the absolute
godhead. He is a luminous statement of unity in
diversity. No matter how many incarnations or
manifestations he may have, Ganesha addresses the
broadest and deepest issues of the human condition.

The Myths Multiply

Praise to the lord Ganesha
Who was invoked through contemplation
by:
Shiva before his victorious battle with
Tripurasura,
Vishnu at the time of constraining Bali,
Brahma as he set out to create the world,
Sheshanaga when he shouldered the burden
of the earth
Parvati before she set out to combat
Mahishasura
Rishis at the beginning of their endeavours
to attain siddhi,
Kamadeva for his victory over the entire
world.
May that lord Ganesha sustain us.

Ganesha caught the imagination of the people. The myths multiplied, fuelled by popular imaginings that endowed him with human qualities and transformed him into the most lovable and accessible of the gods. Stories in various Puranas, which narrate the sacred history of Ganesha, develop the persona of popular perception. Colourful tales of his escapades present him as a fun-loving, pot-bellied god, full of mischief, wit and wisdom, and perpetually hungry.

Human and humorous elements were cleverly combined in the myths to create a genial deity with whom his devotees could easily identify, while symbols and allegories imparted glimpses of the intangible. To early societies, these myths were also an important method of instruction—a crucial tool of religion developed to focus attention and to communicate important insights as well as lessons on social and moral values. But above all, the myths are entertaining, beguiling stories that have enthralled Ganesha's devotees for centuries.

Several myths describe his life with his parents and his brother Kartika whom he constantly bests.

Kartika (also known as Subramanya or Skanda) was handsome as an angel and strong as a thunderbolt, but smug and rather stuffy. Ganesha with his elephant head and plump, pot-bellied body suffered in contrast. But in due course he rose above his physical limitations. He excelled in the arts and grew especially fond of music and dancing. He came to be known as a gay, carefree young man, devoted to the good things in life.

Kartika, on the other hand, excelled in the martial arts and became the commander of the celestial armies. As the boys grew up, Parvati was anxious to see them married before her husband retreated again into meditation and asceticism. When she discussed this with Shiva, he expressed his desire that his sons should travel around the earth to see the world and to gain insights into its peoples before they married. Besides, those that performed this pilgrimage earned punyam, religious merit. The parents debated their divergent priorities and finally arrived at the idea of a race around the world between their two sons. The one who completed the arduous journey first would be married before the other.

The proposal suited Kartika's athletic disposition. After receiving his parents' blessings, he mounted his peacock and set off on the journey. He journeyed rapidly through beautiful woods and across high mountains. He met many people and bore witness to their sorrows and joys. And while he travelled, he often thought of his brother and pitied his inability to travel as fast as himself.

Ganesha, however, was well aware of his
limitations. He knew that his portly frame
would burden his vehicle, the mouse, and
that the journey would take him more than
half his lifetime. On pondering the problem
he found a solution. A pilgrimage around
the earth, he realized, could not possibly
gain him as much religious merit as a
pradakshina (circumambulation) of his
divine parents.

So he approached Shiva and Parvati, bowed
to them respectfully, touched their feet
affectionately and walked around them
seven times, making seven obeisances,
offering them flowers and sandal paste, and
chanting mantras. The celestial parents
were puzzled and urged Ganesha not to
waste so much time, but to attempt to catch
up with Kartika on his pilgrimage round
the world. Ganesha continued to chant
'pitrudevo bhava, matrudevo bhava' while
bowing to them and offering more flowers.
Finally, after the seventh circumambulation
of his parents, Ganesha told them, 'My
journey around the world is complete.'

He addressed Shiva, 'O most respected

father, the Vedas are at the tip of your
tongue. You are the embodiment of all that
is sacred on earth and in heaven. And the
scriptures declare "pitrudevo bhava",
consider your father as your god.' Then
Ganesha turned to Parvati, 'O dearest
mother, you are the embodiment of shakti,
the dynamic energy of the universe. A
pradakshina around one's parents is of
greater significance than a pradakshina
around the earth. Since I have performed
seven pradakshinas of you, my revered
parents, I have already attained sevenfold
merit. I now desire to stay here and to serve
you as your dutiful son.'
Shiva and Parvati were moved by their
son's devotion and his wisdom. They
decided that his maturity indicated that he
was ready for marriage and initiated the
search for an appropriate wife.

This myth is a charming illustration of the
manner in which folk imaginings invested the gods
with the feelings and passions of common men.
Ganesha's supreme filial devotion holds him up as
a model of the dutiful son, to which all sons, the

myth implies, should aspire. A touchstone for family values, this myth also endorses by implication the paramount importance of parents as the source and sustenance of Hindu family life. Devotees smile, during its recounting, at the craftiness of their god, who found such a wise solution to a race he was certain to lose. Indeed, this story is one of the foundations for Ganesha's association with wisdom, an attribute further accentuated in the story of the *Mahabharata*. At a more philosophical level, its primary message is that bhakti, or love that is devotion, is the most effective path to salvation. Meanwhile the story continues . . .

Vishvarupa Prajapati, who ruled over a part of the Himalayas, not too far from Mount Kailasha, had two lovely and most accomplished daughters—Siddhi and Buddhi. He heard of the search for a bride for Ganesha and dispatched his family priest to offer his two daughters in marriage. The match was arranged and the wedding was conducted with pomp and ceremony. Celestial dancers performed with sublime grace while singers sang their sweetest airs before the distinguished gathering of gods

and goddesses, sages and holy men, who
all blessed the couple.

In due course of time, a son was born to
each wife, named Labh, gain of the highest
wealth, and Kshema, the complete
protection of that bounty.

When Kartika returned triumphant from his
journey around the world and found he had
been tricked by his brother, he was furious.
He vowed eternal celibacy and stomped off
to the Krauncha mountains, where he lives
to this day.

The race between the brothers is a popular
metaphor and is retold with several variations.
Another version of the myth has both brothers falling
in love with Siddhi and Buddhi, and embarking on
a race to win the ladies. Other variations change
the impetus to a dispute over an apple or a bowl of
the sweet modakas.

Yet another myth recounts how Brahma gave
Ganesha his wives.

After the dissolution of the universe,
Brahma, drifting in the primordial waters
that preceded creation, came across

Ganesha sitting in a lone banyan tree that remained. Ganesha touched Brahma's head and initiated him into the mantra 'Om'. Brahma prayed before Ganesha who bestowed upon him the knowledge to create the universe, in return for which he gave Ganesha his two wives, representative of prudence and prosperity.

Stories such as these are the product of a people who lived in a constant dialogue with myth, from time to time adding details to further clarify a point or just to accommodate other deities, such as Brahma and Kartika.

Siddhi and Buddhi symbolize the attainments that worshippers of Ganesha aspire towards. They are also seen as the energies of Ganesha, through whom he is able to work such wonders for his devotees. But in none of the legends do either of them really acquire a persona. They are uni-dimensional and only representative of certain aspects of Ganesha. They are frequently depicted fanning the elephant-headed god and are often referred to simply as dasis, attendants. Sometimes one is shown seated on Ganesha's left thigh with a bowl of flat sweet modakas in her lap, from which

Ganesha helps himself with his trunk.

Ganesha's marriage and his progeny also enlarge the context of his worship. He is often addressed by devotees who are unable to beget children. The Ganesha Nataraja temple at Madurai, for example, is frequented by childless couples. It is believed that the god will grant them children if they bathe his image and circumambulate it every morning for forty-eight days. In parts of North India, women observe a vrata to bear sons. They fast until moonrise and worship at a Ganesha temple on the fourth day, or Chaturthi, of the bright half of the lunar month, especially in the month of *Magha*, when couples also come together to worship Ganesha.

The fact that Ganesha is married is an important reinforcement of the attributes of fertility associated with him. In Bengal, the story is told of his wedding with the banana tree. Given his appearance, Ganesha was almost unmarriageable. The mute and uncomplaining banana bride was his last and only hope. The tree is called the kela bau and is ritually transformed into the goddess, during the autumnal worship of Durga in Bengal. A young banana plant wrapped in a sari is placed next to an image of Ganesha throughout the ritual. The drooping and rustling leaves of the plant and its swaying movement suggest a coy and veiled girl bride, while connotations of fertility ascribed to the plant enrich similar associations with Ganesha. There is also of course the elephant's fondness for the fruit and juicy stem of the plantain.

Ganesha is frequently depicted with Saraswati, the goddess of learning and music, and Lakshmi, the goddess of wealth and prosperity. Since Ganesha is associated with similar attributes as the goddesses, many devotees believe that they were his wives in previous incarnations. This assumption is reinforced by their worship along with Ganesha, especially during Diwali. But no myths support this notion. The deities are worshipped together simply because they represent similar goals.

According to some myths, Ganesha is not even married. In fact, he is often described as a celibate, indeed as the lord of brahmacharins. A delightful legend from South India explains that he is a bachelor.

When Shiva and Parvati wanted Ganesha to marry, he insisted that he would only wed a woman as beautiful and accomplished as his mother. The heavens were scoured for such a paragon, but in vain, and Ganesha came down to earth to continue his search. That is why images of Ganesha are found in every roadside temple, by a pond or a water tank, or in the hollows of trees on the outskirts of villages. He is still looking.

Ganesha and his ganas were originally regarded as celibates, in keeping with their status as followers of Shiva, the supreme ascetic. But in many parts of India there are images of Ganesha, his wives and sons, all living together in his celestial kingdom Svaanda Dhama, the abode of bliss. His magnificent palace situated on the 'wish jewel' island, encircled by a 'forest of wish-fulfilling trees', is surrounded by the 'ocean of sugar cane juice'. Ganesha sits on a lotus made up of the letters of the alphabet, indicating his wisdom and learning, and the lotus rests on his lion throne, borrowed from his mother.

There is a marvellous playfulness in this description of Ganesha's home, that is the product of a more childlike, perhaps truer time, when impulse was unrestrained, when it was possible to conceive of a magical world, a world that never was and always will be.

Ganesha's kingdom has four gates, each guarded

by two of his eight special attendants, Paarshadaas, who are probably adaptations of the eight Dikpalas, the guardians of the directions in Hindu tradition. Like Ganesha, they are all short, four armed— signifying their multiple powers—and the tip of their index finger touches the thumb in a mudra which signifies their soul's unity with god.

Also in residence at Ganesha's kingdom is his mouse, given to him, according to one story, as a birth gift by the earth. Another version explains that Ganesha's mouse is actually Agni, god of fire.

> Once there was a great feud between Agni and the other gods. Tension mounted till the god of fire finally assumed the form of a mouse and disappeared into the earth. The conflict was resolved over the years and the gods gave the mouse to Shiva to energize him through the powers of Agni to create his son, Kartika. The purpose served, Shiva then gifted the mouse to his eldest son Ganesha who for a long time had been without a mount.

Ganesha's riding of the lowly mouse is also said to symbolize the taming of the ego by knowledge, a goal enjoined upon the faithful in many sacred writings. Indeed, the scriptures explain that control of the ego implies the attainment of expanded consciousness. An allegorical story explains this edict in simpler terms.

> Gajamukha, the giant elephant-headed demon, terrorized the three worlds, secure in the knowledge that a boon he had obtained protected him from gods and demons, men and beasts. Since Ganesha was beyond these categories, as half-god and half-elephant, the devas sent him to do battle with the demon. In the heat of combat Ganesha broke off his right tusk and threw it as a spear at his enemy. The tusk struck Gajamukha with tremendous force. He crashed to the ground and transformed himself into a giant mouse. Ganesha immediately leapt on the back of the mouse and subdued it—and has ever since used it as his vehicle.

Simple stories such as these from India's rich spiritual and mystic traditions taught the people all they needed to know to live in harmony despite differences, to seek unconventional means of compromise and assimilation.

Ganesha's widespread appeal gains much from his essential humanness. Several myths dwell upon this aspect of his persona, spinning out elaborate stories. Far from being a perfect god who is unattainable and worshipped from afar, Ganesha is often mischievous, a quality which specially endears him to devotees.

Once, while passing the great ocean of milk, Ganesha couldn't resist dipping his trunk into it. He sucked and sucked until he had swallowed the entire ocean, including Vishnu, Brahma, Lakshmi and Garuda. And then like a child, he spat out all he had drunk. Vishnu and his companions were thrown violently onto the ground. When Vishnu regained his composure, he found that he had lost his conch. Just then he heard its wondrous tones resonate through the universe and realized that one of Ganesha's ganas had it. He asked Shiva to intervene. Shiva advised Vishnu to propitiate Ganesha by building a shrine for him at Kanchipuram; only then would his conch be returned.

Ganesha's actions in this myth tread the fine line between wickedness and mischief and display some of the early demonic undertones associated with the deity. The most common myth about Parvati's creation of Ganesha presents his rebirth as a result of his beheading by Shiva. Ganesha's very being, therefore, is a consequence of discord. Disharmony, a natural corollary, characterizes such mischief-making episodes.

In fact, on one occasion, Ganesha actually created a demon himself.

Once, when Shiva reduced Kama, the god of love, to ashes with the fiery energy of his third eye, Ganesha playfully gathered the embers up, moulded them into a figure and breathed life into his creation. Thus the terrible demon Bhandasura was born. Fortified by a boon obtained from Shiva, whom he had propitiated, Bhandasura proceeded to harass the inhabitants of the three worlds. Such was his power that Durga-Parvati had to battle with him for nine nights and nine days before she finally killed him on the evening of the tenth day.

Undertones of discord and conflict persist in this myth. It especially recalls the strife between Ganesha's divine parents. The son creates a demon, who obtains a boon from the father and can only be killed by the mother. The inherent psychological tensions present in this story (and indeed in the persona of Ganesha himself) recall familial myths from other cultures and other times, demonstrating incontrovertibly that the world's peoples are more alike than different and that concepts such as these derive from the childhood of humankind.

Conscious of the contradictions inherent within their patron deity, Ganesha's devotees developed myths to explain his proclivity towards good as well as evil. The following story marks the transition of Ganesha from a malignant to a benevolent deity.

Once, King Abhinanda was performing a great sacrifice. But he forgot to set aside a share of the offerings for Indra. Enraged at this insult, Indra called upon Kala Purusha and ordered him to disrupt the proceedings. Kala took the form of Vighnasura, killed the king and began to impede the peformance of pious deeds. Deeply concerned at the subversion of righteousness, the sage Vashishtha and others beseeched Brahma to intervene. Brahma directed them to Ganesha, who alone had the power to destroy Kala Vighnasura. Ganesha easily defeated the demon. Begging for mercy, Vighnasura threw himself at the deity's feet and promised that henceforth he would serve Ganesha and obey all his commands. As a token of his subservience, he begged Ganesha to assume the title of Vighnaraja, lord of obstacles. Since that day, if Ganesha is not propitiated before a ritual, Vighnasura appears and causes disruption.

Vighnasura thus works on behalf of Ganesha as Vighnaraja, creating impediments in worship if the deity is not properly honoured. The negative role of placing obstacles is now no longer shouldered by Ganesha. Instead, it is ascribed to the demon who serves him into eternity. Several other myths however continue to expand on Ganesha's continued proclivity to create difficulties. A favourite story tells of Vishnu's wedding with Lakshmi.

'All the gods had been invited to the wedding except Ganesha, because Vishnu felt that his pot-bellied corpulence would detract from the splendour of the wedding party. Narada muni, the Puranic harbinger of bad tidings, in his usual role of troublemaker, informed Ganesha of his exclusion. Furious, Ganesha ordered his mouse to contrive a labyrinth of burrows under the wheel of Vishnu's chariot. Predictably, it sank into the riddled ground. Such was the weight of the chariot and so vast the network of burrows that it became impossible to move the wheel. It dawned on Vishnu that the burrows must have been made by Ganesha's mouse, at the bidding of the slighted deity. He invoked Ganesha and apologized to him. Mollified, the elephant-headed deity was persuaded to attend the festivities and all went well.

This whimsical little story not only warns of dire consequences if Ganesha is affronted, it also establishes his status over Vishnu. Even the great god must propitiate Ganesha. On one occasion Ganesha even bests his father Shiva. A myth from South India elaborates.

During an exceptionally hot summer, the world was devoured by drought. Sage Agastya went to Shiva to plead for water just when the river goddess Kaveri was worshipping the lord. Shiva put her into Agastya's waterpot and assured him there would be no more shortages. Indra, the god of rain, grew indignant at Shiva's interference in his realm of activity and persuaded Ganesha to upset Agastya's pot. Unable to resist an opportunity for some fun, Ganesha, disguised as a crow, flew onto the edge of the pot and spilt the water.

Moved by Agastya's great distress, however, Ganesha revealed himself in the spilled water, refilled the sage's waterpot and assured him that the Kaveri would always flow for the nourishment of mankind. Ganesha also promised that he would always be present in the waters of the river to provide spiritual sustenance.

Although Ganesha thus establishes his dominance over both Shiva and Indra, he also indirectly aids his father by establishing a continuous source of nourishment, both material and spiritual, in the river Kaveri. The mischief is balanced by responsible action.

The Ganapatayas, who regarded Ganesha as the supreme deity, developed legends to establish his supremacy. A popular myth describes how Ganesha demonstrated his superiority over the three great gods.

> In order to teach the gods a lesson in humility and to demonstrate his ultimate power, Ganesha once permitted Tripurasura to conquer the three worlds. Girded by the power of Ganesha, the demon quickly subjugated Brahma and Vishnu. He then tackled Shiva and instructed him to descend from his home on Mount Kailasha. Shiva rushed to seek the protection of Ganesha. He paid obeisance to his son, imploring him to save them from Tripurasura. Shiva's faith touched Ganesha. He empowered his father to vanquish the demon and save the three worlds.

The message is clear. Ganesha is the Supreme Reality, bountiful and eternal. He brings well-being to the entire universe, destroying all evil. Just as he strengthened Shiva's resolve and enhanced his abilities, so too does he invest his followers with determination, self-confidence and the will to succeed.

Other myths enlarge Ganesha's realm of influence. They describe how he maintains the reign of righteousness by placing hurdles in the way of the greedy, be they gods or men, and also before those who do not worship him or his father.

When the gods churned the cosmic ocean, they were so eager to obtain amrita, the elixer of immortality, that they forgot to invoke Ganesha or his father Shiva. Suddenly poison began to spew out of the primordial waters, threatening to engulf the universe and even the heavens. The gods and demons fled to Brahma. Unable to help, he took them to Vishnu, who in turn directed them to Shiva. Shiva explained that the spread of poison was in punishment for their heedless disregard of himself and his son.

An evident add-on to the ancient samudra manthana myth which describes the churning of the ocean, this story seeks to grant Ganesha greater legitimacy.

Centuries slipped by and with each passing year, devotees dreamt up innumerable new permutations and combinations of the Ganesha story so as to encompass other personae from the vast body of Hindu myth. Thus, the tale is told of Ganesha creating impediments to prevent Ravana from carrying away a precious and sacred Shivalinga.

> Ravana, as everyone knows, was a great devotee of Shiva. He meditated upon the great god and beseeched him to come to Lanka to make his kingdom completely invincible. When Shiva demurred, Ravana attempted to lift Mount Kailasha and move it bodily to his capital, but Shiva crushed him with his finger. Ravana sought his mercy and performed severe penance. Eventually Shiva relented and gave him one of the twelve jyotirlingas, cautioning him not to place it on the ground, for if he did so, the linga would become rooted to that place forever.
>
> Ravana set off with the linga, delighted that he would deprive a large number of Shiva's

devotees of the opportunity of worship. Wanting the linga back, the gods turned to Ganesha for help. The elephant-headed deity prevailed upon Varuna, god of water, to enter Ravana's belly and cause his bladder to fill. Meanwhile, Ganesha disguised himself as a cowherd and began to loiter near Ravana. The demon came to trust his new companion and gave him the linga to hold while he relieved himself. Ganesha immediately placed the linga on the ground and it took root.

And however much Ravana pulled at the linga, exerting all his legendary might, it could not be moved.

Hence its name Mahabaleshwar. All the tugging, however, caused the linga to become slightly elongated rather like the shape of a cow's ear, from which derives another name: Gokarnam.

Enraged at the loss of the linga, Ravana then turned to Ganesha and hit him, creating a dent on the icon of the deity which is visible even today at the Mahabaleshwar temple in northern Karnataka.

Several myths dwell on the tricks that Ganesha played to force the righteous King Divodasa of Kashi to leave his capital so that Shiva and Parvati could dwell there in seclusion. Elements of unfairness on Ganesha's part, in the various renditions of the tale, are countered by the fact that his actions are always at the behest of his divine father.

> In order to carry out Shiva's instructions to vacate Kashi, Ganesha devised a plan. He appeared in a dream to a low caste barber, Kantaka, and asked him to build a temple dedicated to him. When the shrine was completed, many devotees were blessed with sons and with great riches. Ganesha granted all earthly desires to those that propitiated him. Only the queen's repeated prayers for a son remained unanswered by Ganesha, who hoped to thus arouse King Divodasa's anger. Predictably, the king became enraged at Ganesha. In his fury, he destroyed the shrine, enabling Ganesha to curse him and the city of Kashi, which consequently became deserted. Then Shiva and Parvati took up residence in their favourite city.

Ganesha tricks the king to remove an impediment for Shiva. He prompts, in fact induces, the king's ire and sacrilegious action, which in turn enables him to oust Divodasa. Does the end then justify the means?

There is another version of the same story.

Out of his own body, Ganesha created a Brahmin, Dhundi, whom he instructed to delude the people of Kashi with Buddhist teachings. He also summoned Vishnu and told him to assume the form of a Buddhist monk, to mislead the citizens of Kashi as well as the royal couple. Dhundi and Vishnu were successful in their task and converted the people to Buddhism, leading them to abjure sacrifice and temple ritual. The citizens' neglect of their religious duties brought upon them the terrible consequences of divine wrath, which ultimately forced the people of Kashi to abandon their city.

This story, from the period when Buddhism was flourishing, is an interesting commentary on the times. Thousands flocked to the new faith, eroding the numbers of those who still worshipped the Hindu gods. The myth warns of the dangers of conversion and reiterates the importance of ritual and sacrifice (forbidden by the Buddha), which, if neglected, would provoke the fury of the gods.

The South Indian rendering of this story is less complicated.

> Ganesha arrived in Kashi disguised as an astrologer and caused the people to have bad dreams. Then, interpreting their dreams in conjunction with the position of the stars, he hinted at the impending ruin of their city. The people abandoned Kashi in fear leaving it free for Shiva and Parvati.

Another version resolves the moral dilemma associated with the need to dislodge Divodasa from Kashi: it describes the king as a dreadful demon whom Ganesha had to assume fifty-six different forms to vanquish.

Many myths describe Ganesha using his supreme powers to aid his devotees in every situation and to allow them to realize even the most impossible dreams, provided they worship him. Thus there is

the story of the famous warrior king Vishwamitra
and the Brahmin Vashishtha.

When Vishwamitra saw the powers of sage
Vashishtha, he was jealous and desired to
become a Brahmin, which of course is an
impossible task for a Kshatriya. He
meditated and prayed, performed penance
and practised asceticism, but his goal eluded
him. Then he went to Mount Kailasha to
lord Shiva, who taught him how to address
Ganesha since he alone could remove the
impediments that hindered the achievement
of Vishwamitra's desire. Vishwamitra
worshipped Ganesha with a fervent heart
and the impossible became possible—he
became a Brahmin.

Anything can be achieved with the deity's
benediction. Ganesha is not difficult to please. He
is easily moved to come to the aid of those who
invoke him with a pure heart. True worship of
Ganesha can lead to the cure of moral as well as
physical ills and is even believed to liberate devotees
from the karmas of past lives.

King Somakanta of Devanagara was afflicted with leprosy and retired to a forest. There he encountered sage Bhrigu, whom he asked for a cure. The sage told the king that in a previous life he had been negligent and cruel. It was his bad karma that had caused him to become a leper. But later, the sage explained, the king had repented for his misdeeds. In recompense, he had spent his fortune to refurbish an abandoned Ganesha temple. Pious deeds, even of a previous life, especially those related to the service of Ganesha, carry great merit. Bhrigu therefore cured the king by reciting the 108 names of the elephant-headed deity while sprinkling holy water on him.

To the faithful, stories such as these are harbingers of hope: for surely, if the great god is moved to perform such miracles by so simple a penance, how can he ignore the simpler petitions of everyday life?

Ganesha's curative powers are evoked in many other myths, including one from Nepal which presents him as Surya Vinayaka.

Once there was a pious Brahmin who lived west of Doleshvara with his only son, whom he loved beyond life itself. The boy frequently wandered into the forest nearby, collecting wild herbs for the family. One day, he met with a sudden death. The devastated father invoked Pashupati Shiva and begged him to revive his son. Shiva told the Brahmin to go to the sacred grove at Prakanda, where Ganesha appeared in a ray of sunlight, dazzling in his beauty. The Brahmin prostrated himself before the apparition and when he arose, he found his son restored to life.

Everything is possible through Ganesha, even the reversal of death, providing the devotee surrenders completely at his feet.

In addition to his supreme powers, Ganesha is also popularly associated with wisdom and learning. These attributes appear in the legend about the composition of the *Mahabharata*, which also establishes Ganesha's status as the patron deity of writers and students.

When the famous Brahmin scholar-sage

Krishna Dvaipayana, better known as Vyasa, decided to compose the epic *Mahabharata*, he approached Brahma and told him of his desire to write the longest poem in the world. He requested Brahma to help him find an accomplished scribe. Brahma suggested Ganesha, whose help was needed for all great endeavours, and who, moreover, could remove all obstacles to the creative process. Ganesha agreed to write the epic, but added the ingenious condition that Vyasa compose continuously and without a pause. Vyasa, who recognized the potential trickery, added the provision that Ganesha write each couplet only after he had fully comprehended its entire meaning.

The bargain made, Vyasa found that Ganesha was still writing too fast for him to compose new thoughts. Therefore he dictated some couplets, still found in the epic today, which have as many as 108 meanings. These forced Ganesha to pause and ponder, giving the sage time to devise the next series of couplets. Despite Ganesha's injunctions, it took the duo three years to

complete the one hundred thousand couplets
that make up the great epic.

Scholars agree that this myth is a relatively
recent interpolation and point out that there is no
other significant mention of Ganesha in the entire
Mahabharata. Indeed, many believe that the
Ganesha–Vyasa story reflects an attempt to include
the elephant-headed deity in the epic, in order to
enhance his standing, because it is said that if
something is not mentioned in the *Mahabharata*, it
does not exist.

The persona of Ganesha as the patron deity of
writers is further strengthened in the myth in which
sage Bhrigu, while narrating the Ganesha Purana
to King Somakanta, describes how the text came to
be composed.

In very early times, there was originally
only a single Veda. The great sage Vyasa
separated it into four sections, but he found
these were still too complex. To make their
meaning more accessible to the common
people, he decided to write the Puranas.
While doing so, he kept losing the thread
of his thoughts and forgetting the stories he

had composed in his mind. Brahma explained to Vyasa that his difficulties arose from his neglect of Ganesha. He pointed out that Vyasa had not even begun any of his verses with an invocation to the patron god of writers. The sage asked Brahma to tell him more about Ganesha, and so Brahma narrated the Ganesha Purana.

There are also many lighter aspects to the personality of the elephant-headed deity. Despite his bulk, Ganesha is an accomplished dancer like his father. He is also the mridangam player of the gods and the patron deity of tabla players. The story goes that the tabla was created when Shiva once got very angry with Ganesha.

One day Ganesha was pounding on his mridangam with rather too much enthusiasm. Shiva could not bear the noise and in anger broke it into two with his trident, creating the split tabla.

The father and son evidently settled their differences later, for elsewhere Ganesha is described playing the mridangam in the celestial orchestra, while Shiva danced in ecstasy.

Although Ganesha is the deity of all musicians, he is held in special reverence by those who play the mridangam. Many recite a dhyana of Ganesha and follow it up with phases of percussion. In addition to the talas or rhythms associated with Brahma and Shiva, there are also some named for Ganesha, such as the Gaja prana and the Ganesha prana or Gaja prabandha.

Over the years, Ganesha continued to grow in stature and popularity. He even challenged his divine mother.

Once Parvati was out hunting deer with her son. She took careful aim, but just as she was about to release the arrow, Ganesha knocked against her arm. This happened repeatedly. Parvati turned to him in exasperation. He smiled, and reminded her, 'Mother, you have forgotten to invoke your son. Before you take aim you must utter "Om Shri Ganesha namaha". Then and only then will your arrow reach its target.'

Women all over India perform vratas in honour of various gods, during which they observe fasts

and perform rituals. But irrespective of the deity
that the ritual addresses, the fast cannot be broken
without telling a story about Ganesha and invoking
the particular manifestation of his benevolence
described in the story. Many describe extraordinary
adventures, which, of course, are really tests of
devotion. Several stories focus on couples, where
only one of the two is a devotee of Ganesha. One
such story is about a pair of frogs.

> The female frog was a great devotee of
> Ganesha and constantly uttered his name.
> Her husband was frequently irritated by her
> devotions and often told her that as a good
> wife she should be chanting his name and
> not that of some deity. But the lady frog,
> unperturbed, continued with her devotions.
> One day, the king's men came to the pond
> to collect water for their cooking pot. The
> frogs were scooped up in their vessel and
> put on the fire to boil. Realizing that divine
> intervention was desperately needed, the
> male frog asked his wife to invoke
> Ganesha's help. She reminded him, 'But my
> husband, you told me not to.' He
> apologized and begged her to pray for their

lives. As soon as the female frog uttered
Ganesha's name, two bulls began to fight.
Their fierce combat brought them near the
pot on the fire. They knocked it over and
the frogs hopped back to the pond.

'As you helped the frog who remembered you
O Ganesha,' chant the women, 'so too be pleased to
help us when we call upon you, O lord.'

And as they listen to the myth, the women
acquire its energies, strengthen their resolve and
buttress their faith.

Yet another vrata story reminds devotees that
Ganesha is always moved by true devotion and
rewards it with gifts of great prosperity. It is also an
allegory of the soul's journey towards enlightenment,
which is ultimately what Ganesha helps mankind
to achieve.

Once there was a fair honouring Ganesha
near a temple outside a village. A little girl
pestered her mother to let her join her
friends who had all gone to participate in
the festivities. Eventually her mother agreed
and gave her daughter two churma laddoos,
'Feed one to Ganesha,' she told her

daughter, 'and then eat the other yourself.'
The little girl went straight to the Ganesha
temple, offered a laddoo to the deity, and
settled down in front of the image waiting
for him to eat the offering. Hours passed
and dusk approached. The little girl refused
to leave until Ganesha ate her laddoo. She
waited and waited. Eventually Ganesha,
moved by her devotion, manifested himself
before her and she fed him the laddoo.

Then she grabbed one of his hands and
refused to release her hold. Ganesha said
that he would grant her whatever she wished
if she let him go. The little girl remembered
the old saying: when offered a boon, ask
for benefits that will extend over three
generations. So she said, 'I want to see my
grandson eating from a gold katori in a
palatial haveli where I am surrounded by
seven sons and seven daughters-in-law. My
husband is with me and together we watch
our grandchildren playing.' And so indeed
it was.

Ganesha is kind-hearted, always ready to help
the weak and the poor. Though prone to anger, he

is always just. His reputation for these qualities take a comic form in a folktale about two neighbours—one rich and the other poor.

> One day the poor neighbour and his wife worshipped Ganesha in their home, with offerings of sesame seeds and sugar. In the middle of the night, they were awakened by a voice. 'I am pleased with you,' it said. When the couple asked who it was, the voice replied, 'It is I, Chauth Gosain,' meaning Ganesha. Suspecting that the voice might actually belong to a thief, the wife asked what the intruder wanted. He inquired where he might relieve himself. Terrified, the couple told him to use the corner of the room. When the first light of day appeared, the frightened couple found piles of gold and jewels in the corner and deeply regretted that they had treated the god so discourteously.
>
> The poor couple became rich overnight. And when the rich neighbour asked how this had come about, the couple told him of the occurrences of that miraculous night.
>
> The rich neighbour listened intently to the

story and inquired in detail about the
procedures of worship the poor man had
followed to achieve such impressive results.
Soon thereafter, the rich man and his wife
worshipped Ganesha in exactly the same
way. In the middle of the night, the same
voice made the same request. The rich
couple gladly invited the intruder to relieve
himself in the corner of the room. But when
dawn broke, the couple was dismayed to
find their room filled with human
excrement, flooded with urine and giving
forth a horrible stench.

No one can fool Ganesha. He is easily pleased,
but only if there is sincerity in the devotion; there
will be unexpected rewards for the humble, and just
retribution for the arrogant. The folktale also
endorses the belief that desire, in this case for riches,
can never be sated.

One more story dwells on Ganesha's particular
compassion for the poor with typical soul-enriching
wisdom.

One day Ganesha was seized with a longing
to eat kheer (rice porridge). He disguised

himself and set off, armed with a pinch of rice and sugar, and a teaspoon of milk. He presented these to everyone he met and asked them to make him some kheer. Only an old lady took pity on the hungry lad. She brought out a small katori and prepared to put the ingredients in it to cook the sweet-dish. Ganesha asked her to put them in a large pot. She tried to explain that it was unnecessary, but to please him she did as he asked. And of course, as the kheer cooked, it filled the pot.

While the rice and milk cooked, Ganesha went for a walk. But the kheer was ready long before he returned. The smell was mouth-watering and the old lady couldn't resist tasting the kheer. But before she did so, she invoked Ganesha in her mind, inviting him to partake of the kheer. One spoonful led to another, till she had eaten almost half the pot. Ganesha returned. The old lady invited him to eat, but Ganesha replied, 'I have already eaten the kheer.' Then he appeared before her in all his celestial glory and showered her with gifts.

Myths are also blueprints for an ideal life. In this story, for example, only the old lady had compassion, only she had belief and true devotion— virtues that the devout must emulate.

Some of the best stories about Ganesha are the utterly down-to-earth ones with no epic dimensions or grand morals. These are playful stories about simple folk, and a god who becomes one of them:

Once there was an old woman whose son married a virtuous and beautiful girl. He left his wife at home with his mother while he travelled far away to earn his living. Now the mother-in-law, as do so many mothers-in-law, maltreated the young bride and gave her scarcely enough to eat. The young woman was always so hungry that she took to raiding the larder every night. But she always scattered some of the food about, and when her mother-in-law discovered the mess, she would say, 'It must be the rats.'

This went on for many months, till the rats went to Ganesha and complained that the young woman was giving them a bad name. Ganesha told them to go ahead and seek

vengeance. Now one day, the young woman
removed her sari and went to take a bath.
Her husband returned unexpectedly and
knocked at the door. She hastened out of
the bathing chamber to put on her sari, only
to discover the garment was missing. Her
husband knocked repeatedly and when she
explained that she could not open the door
because her sari, which was there a moment
ago, had vanished, he became suspicious
and angry.

Suddenly, it dawned on her that it must be
the rats taking their revenge. She begged
Ganesha for his intercession and promised
to offer him laddoos if he helped her. The
elephant-headed god took pity on her
predicament and instructed the rats to return
her sari. The young woman went on to
become a great devotee of the lord, who
showered her with every happiness.

Through laughter, through fear, through
admiration, through awe as well as elements of
superstitious dread, these folktales endorse Ganesha's
special powers. Stories such as these help people
come closer to the divine and comfort themselves

by asserting the presence of a benevolent and accessible higher power. They sustain the world, and must be renewed from time to time in order to renew society and the self.

Iconography and Worship

Hail to thee of auspicious form, whose
head is crowned with a garland of stars . . .
I adore thy trunk flung up straight in the
joy of the dance, so as to sweep away the
clouds . . .
Destroyer of obstacles, I worship thy snake-
adorned body . . . the treasure house of all
success.

—Kathasaritsagara

Images of Ganesha proliferated as the centuries
went by and a complex iconography evolved to
reflect the multiple facets of this much-loved deity.
All representations of his sacred form follow the strict
rules enshrined in the ancient canons of iconography,
the shilpa shastras. These prescribe every detail of
the depiction of a deity, in painting as well as
sculpture.

In these texts, Ganesha is described as a deity
with the body of a human and the head of an elephant.
One of the tusks is broken. He has a rotund form
with a prominent pot-belly and is red-hued. In his
hands and often even his trunk, he holds various
symbolic objects. When seated, one leg is folded,
the other rests on a footstool, and a variety of food
is spread at his feet. A mouse sits near the food

looking up at the deity, as though asking his permission to partake of the repast.

This familiar iconographic form of Ganesha is not just the product of a set of norms for representation in art. It is also a powerful visual manifestation of religious belief, imbued with philosophical meaning. Complex abstract concepts are depicted through a variety of symbols and thus communicated to the devout. Iconography goes far beyond the obvious for those who seek to contemplate it deeply. Even the most minute detail of an image recalls episodes in the mythical life of the deity and leads to a deeper understanding of the sacred reality he embodies. Each detail is resonant with layers of meaning, a quality that enables Ganesha to be many things to many people.

Ganesha's body is stunted, almost childlike, and conforms to iconographic norms prescribed for a five-year-old male child. These stipulate that the head and torso be noticeably longer than the legs. The childlike aspect is reinforced by a pronounced chubbiness, which elicits an indulgent affection. It also recalls the specially close bond between Ganesha and his mother.

Ganesha is always visualized as an elephant-headed deity. There are no depictions of his form prior to his beheading or even of the episode of the beheading itself. His significance within the Hindu pantheon rests in his rebirth with an elephant head, which is always one-fifth of the body and is a symbol of his immense wisdom. It is frequently white, recalling the divine white elephant Airavata, whose head, according to one myth, was attached to Ganesha's body after his beheading. (The colour white also signifies purity and the peaceful temperament associated with Ganesha in several of his manifestations.) Images of Ganesha within or inspired by the tantric tradition often depict him with multiple heads, normally ranging in number from three to five.

His small but penetrating eyes are said to see the spirit of the divine in all creation and to perceive the essential unity in the diversity of the world. Usually Ganesha's eyes are red, like those of an elephant, with dark pupils, leading to his name Krishnapingaksha, the black-and-red-eyed one. While in some early sculpture the eyes are depicted very much like those of an elephant, artisans over the centuries have attempted to give them a more human dimension. The face has been flattened and the eyes positioned towards the front rather than the sides, as would have been normal for an elephant.

The eyes have also become larger, sometimes complete with eyebrows and often carefully contrived to convey a very human compassion, sometimes even a glimmer of amusement. On occasion, the eyes are placed close together, with both pupils near the inner edge, creating an angry, almost enraged, expression. This is a demonic manifestation of Ganesha that recalls his early choleric disposition, which required propitiation. Some icons present Ganesha with a third eye, like his father. The three eyes are said to represent the sun, the moon and fire.

The tilak on his forehead is in the form of Shiva's three-pronged trishul and clearly identifies him as a devotee of his father. It is also said to signify Ganesha's dominance over the three worlds— heaven, earth and the underworld—and to symbolize the three modes of being, satvik (purity), rajasik (passion) and tamasik (inertia), over which he has total control.

gunas?

Ganesha is always depicted with his left tusk broken, hence his popular name Ekadanta, the single-tusked one. Many a story is told of its breaking.

Once Ganesha was returning from his

mother's home astride his mouse, after a particularly sumptuous dinner that had made him even bulkier than he already was. The mouse laboured along till he ran into a large snake lying across the road. Startled, the mouse bolted, and Ganesha fell to the ground in an undignified heap. The moon, in the company of his twenty-seven starry consorts, began to laugh. Infuriated, Ganesha broke off one of his tusks and hurled it at the moon, also cursing the celestial orb to lose its light.

Everyone missed the moon. The gods begged Ganesha to revoke his curse. But once a curse has been pronounced it cannot be taken back, it can only be modified. So Ganesha compromised. Instead of making the moon disappear completely, he caused it to wax and wane. Moreover, he insisted that none look upon it on the day that it had laughed at him. Otherwise, he threatened, they would be accused of a crime they had not committed.

In Indian astrology, the moon is malefic on the fourth day of the bright fortnight of the lunar month of Bhadrapada (August–September), when it is said to subvert man's concentration on God.

To indicate Ganesha's dominance over the moon, he is sometimes shown wearing it as an ornament in his headdress, an element that also recalls the iconography of his father Shiva.

There is another myth associated with Ganesha's broken tusk.

Parashurama, the great Brahmin warrior, once arrived unannounced at Mount Kailasha and demanded an audience with Shiva. Ganesha stopped him at the entrance to the divine mansion and explained, as delicately as he could, that he would have to wait, because Shiva was with Parvati. But Parashurama was anxious to pay homage to Shiva, who had given him the axe with which he had slain armies of Kshatriyas. He tried to push past Ganesha, who stopped him. Infuriated, Parashurama threw his axe at Ganesha. Ganesha saw the axe coming, but since the axe had been given to Parashurama by his father, he did not want to violate its sanctity. So he took the blow on his left tusk which was severed as

a result. From that day on, Ganesha came
to be known as Ekadanta.

Ganesha thus loses his tusk as he dutifully fulfils
his role as the guardian of the entrance to his parents'
chamber. He had earlier lost his head while manfully
guarding the door to Parvati's bath. His role as a
guardian continues to be expressed in the placement
of the images above thresholds of homes as well as
temples, which he shields from the ingress of evil
influences. This placement also ensures that
worshippers address the elephant-headed deity before
entering, thus obtaining his benediction and the
assurance of success.

Other myths associated with the damaged tusk
insist that Ganesha broke it off himself to use either
as a weapon to kill a demon or as a writing
instrument in the inscribing of the *Mahabharata*.
He is also said to have lost his tusk as a result of a
childhood wager with Kartika. In another version,
Ravana is credited with cutting off the tusk.

The broken tusk is often held in one of Ganesha's
hands and is considered to represent the ascetic's
staff, the yoga danda, given to him by Shiva. It
reinforces the ascetic aspect of Ganesha's persona,
a manifestation associated with his father, the

greatest of all yogis. On occasion, the tusk is also held in one of his hands as a writing instrument, recalling Ganesha's status as the god of learning.

The single tusk, as opposed to the more usual pair, is also said to remind the devout that the deity has transcended the limitation of opposites—such as the self and other, likes and dislikes, good and bad—that hold mankind in their thrall. He is dwandwa-ateetha, beyond dualities, attached to neither.

The story of Ganesha's fall from his mouse is also associated with another element of his iconography. For after his fall, the deity picked up the reptile and tied it around his distended belly—which is why he is always depicted with a snake around his midriff, or draped across his torso in replication of the sacred thread that indicates his sacred status. Anthropologists are tempted to see the incorporation of the snake in the iconography of Ganesha as a symbol that commemorates the victory of a tribe with an elephant totem over one that worshipped the snake. Since the snake is also an emblem of fertility, it emphasizes Ganesha's prestige as the lord of prosperity—a connotation further enhanced by the nagas that are often sculpted in friezes in close proximity to icons of Ganesha. These reptiles are also associated with Shiva, and thus signify the bond of shared power between father and son.

According to another interpretation, the snake represents the kundalini, the cosmic energy coiled at the base of the spine. This rises when stimulated by yoga, through seven chakras, or energy centres, to the last one, at the crown of the head, where it merges with the Infinite. Ganesha is muladhara adhipati, lord of the muladhara or root chakra, the first of the seven chakras, through which the kundalini must rise, and therefore presides over the beginning of the process of release.

Many a philosophical message is drawn from Ganesha's elephantine anatomy. His trunk, for example, is said to be an embodiment of his viveka, or prudence. Just as elephants use their trunks to discriminate between succulent morsels and unpalatable foods, so too is Ganesha able to distinguish between reality and illusion. Other analogies compare the elephant's ability to uproot a tree as well as pick up a needle from the ground with its trunk to Ganesha's ability to penetrate the realms of the material as well as the transcendental— an objective towards which human-kind must aspire.

The positioning of the trunk is of considerable significance. In most representations of the deity, it is curved to the left, the side of the body associated with the ida naadi, one of the conduits of the subtle body, associated with the moon. When the trunk is placed to the right, the deity, then called Siddhi Vinayaka, requires very special and carefully structured worship. This is because the pingalaa naadi on the right of the body is associated with the sun and is said to cause destruction if the rules of worship are violated. Images with the trunk straight down are considered rare and special as this posture signifies that the sushumna, the energy channel that runs through the spine past the six chakras, is entirely open—a situation that indicates the easy movement of the kundalini and is a stage aspired to by all yogis. But most special of all are images with the trunk swung right up in the air. This position indicates that the kundalini has reached the sahasra chakra at the crown of the head, signifying the attainment of moksha.

Ganesha's big elephant ears flapping gently symbolize the winnowing away of obstacles. While their movement is also perceived to brush away negativity, their size testifies to his capacity to listen to the eternal truths of Vedanta. His large head

denotes his proficiency in reflecting upon these truths
and also recalls his supreme wisdom.

Although Ganesha is usually depicted with four
arms, some images have as many as fourteen or
even eighteen. To the primitive mind multiple arms
represented supernatural powers and the ability to
do many things at the same time. The more
philosophical see his four arms as symbols of the
four qualities of the mind—manasa (intellect), buddhi
(wisdom), ahamkara (ego) and chitta (consciousness).
Ganesha himself represents the pure consciousness,
the atma, that enables these four aspects to function
in harmony. The four arms are also said to stand
for the four directions and reinforce the belief that
Ganesha controls the world.

In his four hands the elephant-headed deity holds
objects, often interchanged, that identify his
attributes. These symbols form a kind of visual
shorthand easily understood by his devotees. They
have allegorical meanings which communicate the
essence of the deity. The noose and the elephant
goad, the pasa and the ankusha, actually pertain to
elephant trainers. Used to capture wild elephants,
the noose is believed by the devout to arrest delusion,
curb the ego and restrain passion. It also draws the
devotee from worldly entanglements and binds him

to the enduring bliss of the inner self. The goad, too, symbolizes Ganesha's role in prodding his devotees out of their inertia, in urging them on to spiritual quests. According to some, the axe represents the destruction of desire and attachment, while others view it as a symbol of the cutting away of illusion and false reasoning. The sweet modakas represent the rewards of spiritual seeking, while the lotus is synonymous with purity. It also endorses Ganesha's aquatic associations and stature as lord of fertility and prosperity.

The modaka and the lotus, usually held in the two lower hands, are sometimes replaced by stylized hand gestures or mudras—the abhaya mudra indicating reassurance and the vara mudra which communicates the deity's blessings. Ganesha is also sometimes depicted holding objects such as the mace and discus. Usually associated with Vishnu, these reflect Vaishnavaite attempts to claim the popular elephant-headed deity as their own.

Ganesha as a child is also depicted with four arms, in which he holds a mango, a banana, a jackfruit and a stick of sugar cane, all favoured by both children and elephants. In his trunk he often grasps a wood apple, fruit of the bel tree, sacred to Shiva. In these representations, Ganesha is depicted as a cherubic and engaging child.

Even the adult Ganesha has childlike qualities, such as his inability to resist sweets. This, as well as his very human enjoyment of the good things in life, enhances his mass appeal.

A delightful story describes Ganesha as a little boy, gorging on sweets and modakas. His tummy grew larger and larger. So much so that when he bent down to touch his parents' feet, he found that he could not perform the obeisance, because his stomach was in the way.

But there is more to Ganesha's belly than meets the eye. It indicates prosperity, with which he is closely identified. At a metaphysical level Ganesha's pot belly is said to result from his kundalini shakti which has risen up through the power of his yoga to enlarge his belly. Philosophical interpretations view Ganesha's distinctive stomach as a symbol of his ability to digest all experience and conquer all desire.

Another myth explains how Ganesha's stomach expanded to make him Lambodara, the pot-bellied.

> To show off his wealth, Kubera once invited Shiva and Parvati to a banquet. They suggested that he feed Ganesha instead.

Kubera laughed and scornfully declared that
he could feed many children like their son.
At this, Ganesha fell upon the food,
devouring everything, till there was none
left for the other guests. He then started
eating the floral decorations and soon
moved on to the furniture. Ganesha's belly
became enormous, but he was still hungry.
At Kubera's most urgent request for help,
Shiva gave him a handful of roasted rice
and told him to serve it to Ganesha with
humility. Kubera did so and Ganesha's
hunger was immediately satisfied.

This story implies that the material world,
represented by Kubera's feast, cannot bring
satisfaction. Only the consuming of unfulfilled
desires, symbolized by the roasted rice which cannot
germinate, bestows fulfilment.

Although all Hindu deities are offered food,
devotees always feed Ganesha first, offering vast
quantities of fruit and especially the sweet rice or
wheat cake, the modaka. Such is his partiality for
the modaka that Ganesha is also called
Modakapriya. Indeed, it is said that the more
modakas a devotee offers to Ganesha, the more

inclined the deity will be to remove obstacles.

Ganesha's fondness for the modaka goes back to his childhood. Various myths describe Parvati telling her sons how the gods distributed modakas in celebration of their birth because the sweets are said to represent mahabuddhi (great intelligence) and amrita (ambrosia). She describes its qualities: 'Even one who merely smells it is sure to become immortal. He will become learned in the shastras, clever at weapons, knowledgeable in the tantras . . .' According to another version, the modaka is also said to have been the prize for Ganesha and Kartika's legendary race around the world.

To further legitimize Ganesha's partiality for sweets, the modaka is also viewed as a symbol of his affinity for the delectable taste of Vedanta philosophy. Since the sweet is not common all over the country, favourite regional foods are also offered to Ganesha. In Kerala, his hunger is appeased on special occasions by covering the image in appam.

Even Ganesha's mouse is said to have been drawn out of his burrow by the mouth-watering aroma of the modaka. Unable to resist it, the rodent nibbled at this wondrous food, whereupon he became immortal.

The mouse is Ganesha's vahana or mount, and

is usually depicted below the image of the deity. A bas-relief at the Hasti Gupha (the elephant cave) in Orissa depicts a battle between elephants and mice, in which the elephants were victorious. Anthropologists suggest that this narrative carving and the popular iconography of Ganesha mounted on a mouse may represent the subjugation of the tribe with a mouse totem by elephant worshippers.

Be that as it may, rationalizations multiplied to explain the curious iconography. The elephant-headed god taking the tiny mouse for his vahana again emphasizes Ganesha as dwandwa-ateetha, the lord of opposites, the one beyond dualities. The mouse is also said to represent the atman or soul that has its home deep within every being. Ganesha and his mouse, together, are also said to symbolize the many ways in which the deity can vanquish every hindrance. As the elephant forges mightily ahead, trampling upon obstructing vegetation and uprooting trees, the mouse finds its way through the smallest gaps, even into places like locked granaries, so too, for Ganesha's devotees, shall a path be made through every obstructing circumstance.

In the popular perception, the destructiveness of the rat or field mouse, especially its depredations of the harvest, were allegorically curbed by Ganesha who subordinated the rodent as his mount. The damage caused by the mouse is further minimized by the rodent's indirect propitiation as Ganesha's vahana. The association thus validates Ganesha's status as lord of the harvest.

According to one myth, the mouse was really a gandharva.

One day, in the Dwapara yuga a celestial musician, Kruanca gandharva, rushed out of the court of Indra in a great hurry and accidentally collided with sage Vamadeva. Vamadeva was affronted and cursed the gandharva to become a mouse. Kraunca apologized so profusely that Vamadeva was mollified and said he could be a mouse at Parashurama's ashram. One day, Ganesha came across this mouse, which was causing trouble at the ashram. As mice are wont to do, it had gnawed away at stocks of grain and devastated it. To punish it for its misbehaviour, Ganesha threw his noose, caught the mouse, made it into his vehicle and thus curbed its depredations forever.

At yet another level, the mouse is said to

represent greed and desire, which Ganesha symbolically vanquishes by riding it.

When Ganesha was a small boy, his vahana, the mouse, was very big. It became overconfident and decided to kidnap the deity. The little Ganesha understood the mouse's intent. So when he sat on his vahana, he became so heavy that the mouse vomited out all arrogance, lust and greed.

The sacred syllable Om has a special significance in the iconography of Ganesha since its calligraphic form is said to resemble the face of an elephant in profile. The curve of the *A* is seen to depict the head and belly, the arm of the *U* the trunk, and the central section, shaped like an *M*, represents the plate of sweet modaka offered to him. Om is said to be the primordial sound of creation in which everything is contained. It is God and it is Ganesha. Thus Ganesha is the lord of all worlds and all species. The form of Ganesha is said to also be the visual representation of the highest reality, expressed in the holy words 'tat tvam asi', which emphasize that divinity exists in each individual. Ganesha's elephantine head is believed to represent tat or

Brahman, the universal godhead; his human body
tvam, the self; and their joining together signifies
the union of the individual soul with the ultimate
divinity.

In most images, while Ganesha's head is painted
white, his body is red. Red is believed to be the
colour of the muladhara chakra (located near the
genitals). Myth, however, has a more evocative
rationale. One story attributes the red colour of
Ganesha's body to the blood of a demon that he
killed.

> The demon king Sindhu was so powerful
> that he conquered Brahma, Vishnu and
> Shiva, and decreed that he should be
> worshipped as God. Parvati prayed to
> Ganesha, beseeching that he be born to her,
> for she realized that Ganesha contained all
> the gods within him. Ganesha agreed and
> Parvati told Shiva that the agony of the
> universe would end with the incarnation of
> her son, who alone could destroy Sindhu
> and restore righteousness and virtue.
> Ganesha became manifest and challenged
> the demon king. A titanic battle ensued. The
> demon's blood gushed out, splattering

Ganesha, who has been red-bodied ever
since.

The colour red is also variously attributed to a
drop of blood shed during Shiva and Parvati's
intercourse, or to the swallowing of a demon whose
heat caused Ganesha to develop a raging fever. In
fact, many of Ganesha's ritual preferences are
explained in terms of his need to be cooled. Durva
grass, one of his favourites, for example, is said to
be a very cooling substance.

Ganesha is worshipped in many different
manifestations. According to the Ganesha Purana,
the deity assumed fifty-six forms while battling the
king Durasada. These differed according to the
number of heads and the animals used as the deity's
vahanas. Icons of each of these forms were installed
in seven enclosures around the temple of Ganesha
Dhundiraja at Kashi to protect the city. Even today
the worship of these fifty-six forms is advocated and
pilgrimages are performed on the fourth day of the
suklapaksha, the bright half of the lunar month,
especially on the fourteenth day of the suklapaksha
of the month Magha.

Among the more important forms of Ganesha
is Mahaganapati, the most important deity of the

Ganapatayas, who regard this manifestation as the supreme being. Mahaganapati continues to be a popular icon, worshipped by a broad spectrum of devotees and is widely represented in art. This form of Ganesha has ten hands, each holding objects bestowed by ten deities. Among these is the fruit of the citron tree, associated with Shiva, the numerous seeds of which represent creative power. Then there is the sugar cane bow, a gift from Kama, god of love, with an arrow made of a rice shoot which was gifted by the earth. Both connote agricultural fertility. Mahaganapati also holds Varaha's mace and Vishnu's discus. A pot of jewels held in his trunk, Kubera's gift, indicates wealth and the abundance of the good things of life that the deity showers upon his devotees. A consort holds a lotus, emblem of purity, in one hand and embraces the deity with the other, while gods and demons stand in attendance. These elements represent Mahaganapati's ability to perform the functions of all the gods and his supreme dominance over them all.

Another manifestation, particularly popular in Nepal, is Heramba, protector of the weak. This form of Ganesha has five heads, the colours of which closely parallel the five aspects of Shiva—Ishana, Tatpurusha, Aghora, Vamadeva and Sadyojata—

and seem to indicate Heramba's might. Heramba is astride a lion borrowed from his mother, representing royalty and ferocity. One of his ten arms caresses his consort who is seated in his lap. In representations of Ucchista Ganapati, a deity of vama marg, the left-handed path of tantra, the consort is frequently depicted nude. Worship of this manifestation is performed when the supplicant is in a ritually impure or ucchista state, that is, either naked or with remnants of food in the mouth at the time of worship.

Ganapatayas worship Ganesha in conjunction with his consort, for she is his shakti, his creative energy, through and with whom he is able to function. Her presence is also believed to recall the male and the female instincts present within each human being, which must come together to stimulate a powerful creativity.

Still other forms, most usually associated with tantra, include Haridra Ganapati, Navaneeta Ganapati, Swarna Ganapati and Samtana Ganapati. Each is worshipped with special mantras, as well as very specific yantras. These are used in complex rituals, many conducted to seek and receive material boons, especially those associated with sexuality. These forms as well as those of Mahaganapati,

Heramba and Ucchista Ganapati were also associated with the six fearful abhichara rites, whereby a victim can be manipulated to experience an obsessive attraction, be completely subjugated, consumed with jealousy, immobilized, deluded or even killed.

Ganesha is also worshipped as the central dot or bindu of the ritual diagram associated with him. This consists of two rings of lotus petals which enclose three circles and two squares, and is very similar to the famous Srichakra, the potent mystic diagram that represents the goddess.

During the early medieval period, Jains and Buddhists both incorporated Ganesha into their pantheon. The cult of Ganesha travelled with Mahayana Buddhism to distant lands, including Burma, Thailand, Cambodia, Nepal, Tibet, China, Mongolia and Japan, where his worship spread rapidly.

Ganesha has varied aspects within the Buddhist tradition. At one level, he is regarded as an incarnation of the Bodhisattva Avalokiteshwara and deeply revered. At another, he is one of several Hindu deities presented as converts to Buddhism and consequently depicted in a subsidiary role as a guardian of shrines or of mandalas. Yet another

Buddhist tradition conceives of Ganesha as malevolent and obstructive, hence in some Vajrayana and related Buddhist art he is sometimes shown being subdued by Buddhist deities.

A story from Nepal describes Ganesha's conversion to Buddhism as a result of his subjugation by the deity Vighnantaka.

> Once upon a time, a pandit from Odiyan, Adriyacharya, was sitting on his elephant skin on the banks of the river Vagmati, waiting to commence mystic rites directed at gaining the eight magical powers, the ashta siddhi. Ganesha happened to pass by and discovered that his own image was not among the deities honoured by the master. Affronted, he ordered his ganas to disrupt the proceedings. The acharya summoned various powers to his protection. Ganesha called in the putanas and the kataputanas, who are various categories of demonesses. In response, the acharaya brought in the dasa krodhas, the ten furies. Ganesha and his supporters fell back before their fury. Among the krodhas was Vighnantaka who climbed on Ganesha and rode him as his

vahana. Ganesha tried to escape but Vighnantaka overtook him and jumped on his back again. Humbled, Ganesha sought the protection of the acharaya and became a Buddhist. From that time on Ganesha has had a place in the Buddhist pantheon.

Other cults, in China and especially in Japan, regard the deity in a more benevolent aspect, as the one who bestows all material benefits and supernatural powers. Some of these revolve around the dual-bodied Ganesha called Kangi, a popular form in which two elephant-headed figures, one male and the other female, stand face to face in embrace. The feet of the female image are often placed atop those of the male, a position considered to have erotic overtones. This divinity continues to be most commonly addressed with petitions to fulfil material needs. Rituals are long, complicated and expensive, but are regularly conducted even today. Votive placards are still placed on the periphery of Kangi temples, each inscribed with vows to abstain from some pleasurable activity in return for a specified material benefit, often of revitalized sexual prowess and other worldly, though not always moral, petitions.

The cult was initiated in the early seventeenth century when some merchants from Osaka worshipped Kangi-tan and became exceedingly affluent. In gratitude, they made rich gifts to this deity who went on to become a popular focus of devotion. A quaint Japanese myth explains the origin of this dual-bodied Ganesha.

> There was once a mountain called Vinayaka, whose elephant king, Kangi, was ordered by Maheshwara to create impediments for mortals. The Bodhisattva Avalokiteshwara took pity on the plight of human beings and assumed the form of a female elephant. Kangi immediately fell in love with her and wished to enfold her in an embrace. But Avalokiteshwara insisted that Kangi first cease to create obstacles and vow to be a protector of Buddhism. Kangi readily agreed. The female elephant embraced Kangi and the dual-bodied Ganesha came into being.

In Jainism, Ganesha has always been propitiated to obtain desirable things, even by the gods. Svetambara Jains still invoke Ganesha at the beginning of most auspicious ceremonies or new projects. Although icons of Ganesha in Jain temples have close parallels to depictions within the Brahminical tradition, most are placed on door frames and in the basement, or pitha, of temples, which indicates his lesser status as compared to other deities of the Jain pantheon.

Ganesha is also a familiar figure in South-East Asia, especially Thailand, Cambodia, Vietnam and Indonesia. Although many representations of the deity are within the traditional Hindu context and present Ganesha as a guardian of the threshold and remover of obstacles, the elephant-headed deity is also frequently depicted in isolation. As a result, he is worshipped by different sects and castes of Hindus, as well as by Buddhists and Jains. Particularly large images, found in Thailand and Java, much bigger than anything in India, are believed to testify to his great importance in these regions. Though clearly inspired by Indian expressions, most of these icons are not direct copies but adaptations, modified by distinctive regional characteristics such as clothing and ornamentation. Many of these images are more humanized than their Indian counterparts, with the body less stunted and the belly less pronounced.

Within the mainstream Indian tradition,

however, strict ancient canons governing the
depiction of Ganesha's sacred form have ensured
an overall similarity in representations through the
centuries. Ganesha is most commonly depicted
seated, with one leg folded under him, the other
resting on the ground or on a footstool. The leg on
the ground is said to indicate his association with
the material, while the other that is tucked under
him is considered to represent the posture of
meditation and to remind devotees of the importance
of focusing on the supreme reality. This stance,
therefore, implies that pursuit of the material should
be combined with meditation and spirituality in
order to achieve salvation. Ganesha may be seated
on a lotus, a mouse, or a lion. He may also be
depicted standing or dancing, with an infinite variety
of modulations that continue to evolve.

Each depiction of the sacred form of Ganesha is
urgently alive, vital, potent and somehow endearing:
a consummation of the devotion with which
hundreds of generations of skilled hands and
dedicated hearts have created images, in acts of love
and worship.

The representation of the transcendent and
formless godhead was a complex and difficult task
that stretched over long periods of time. Only

painters and sculptors from families of skilled artisans, steeped in the scriptures and the holy texts that governed the depiction of the gods, were entrusted with such momentous labour. Before the actual work commenced, artisans performed rituals to purify their bodies and abstained from any activity that might distract their minds. They lit incense and meditated till they acquired a personal understanding of the deity and felt able to present the true essence of their lord. Girded with humility, they then embarked upon their labour of love, seeking no recognition, but only to honour Ganesha.

Seated, standing or dancing, images of the elephant-headed deity have stimulated special creativity. His portly and often stunted body has received a powerful modelling of form that imbues icons with life and movement. The symmetry and the balance of limbs, the inflection of the body and the fluid lines all contribute to the creation of superlative images that have enchanted generations of devotees. Artisans have revelled in the immense artistic possibilities of the trunk, in particular, to accentuate rhythmic contours and contrive a wonderful harmony of curved forms. Often the trunk is held horizontal for most of its length, its tip curving down gently to rest appropriately on a bowl of sweets, or, in more risqué tantric representations, in the yoni of a consort.

A favourite stance encountered in temples all over India is that of Ganesha dancing. It is possibly inspired by the image of Shiva as the divine dancer. But while Shiva's dance is of cosmic significance incorporating creation and destruction, Ganesha's does not carry such weighty consequence. His is a more playful version, almost rambunctious, appropriate for the mischievous ganas, associated with fun and frolic, whom Ganesha leads. Indeed, the ganas are often portrayed cavorting and playing musical instruments to accompany Shiva's dance. Some myths present Ganesha dancing before his parents to entertain and divert them. Dance, in many cultures, is, of course, a form of prayer which creates a heightened consciousness and elicits energies that call forth the divinity within the self.

The Kashmiri poet Somadeva composed a number of eulogies in honour of the dancing Ganesha, many of which communicate the joyousness that characterizes such images.

> Victory to Ganesha,
> who when dancing makes a shower of stars . . .
> fall like a rain of flowers
> from the sky by the movement of his trunk.

Despite his considerable bulk, images of the dancing Ganesha are saturated with rhythm, movement and a vigorous grace. One foot is placed before the other, with the leg bent at the knee, thrusting the weight of his body forward to create a sense of movement. The head, the torso and the lower body are often ingeniously inclined in different directions to simulate the postures of dance. In the background, there are usually musicians, especially drummers who pound out the accompanying rhythm.

Images of the child Ganesha, partly inspired by and reinforcing the Vaishnava connection which commonly portrays Krishna as an infant, are also popular.

Depending on the context of the image and the myth it recalls, Ganesha is presented with different degrees of clothing and ornamentation, and with headdresses ranging from the crown of matted hair, reminiscent of Shiva's ascetic aspect, to a diadem, symbolizing sovereignty, or a pile of pots, to indicate his association with water and fertility. He is frequently flanked by his consorts Siddhi and Buddhi, who carry sheaves of wheat and maize or baskets of fruit, highlighting Ganesha's role in assuring plenty. Some representations also incorporate images of Lakshmi, goddess of prosperity, Saraswati, goddess of learning, and Kubera, god of wealth, to amplify his various attributes.

In temples dedicated to Ganesha, subsidary images are positioned according to a set of rules. The figure of Gajakarana is usually placed on the left of the image, Siddhi to the right, Gauri to the north, Buddhi to the east, Saraswati to the south, Kubera to the west. Each of the four entrances of the shrine is guarded by a pair of doorkeepers, dwarapalas, with stunted dwarf-like bodies and fierce expressions. In their hands they hold various weapons.

An icon of Ganesha presides over the entrances to most temples dedicated to other important Hindu deities. He is also usually present in a niche at the beginning of the inner circumambulatory path, where he may be invokèd even before the commencement of the initial parikrama. In Shiva temples, there is often a separate shrine to Ganesha in the south-west corner, to protect the temple from the demons that reside in that direction. Since he is also integral to the iconography of Shiva, images of Ganesha are an inherent part of temple friezes that portray episodes from the life of the great god. Even bronze statues of Shiva usually incorporate a small figurine of Ganesha—an association that endorses both Ganesha's paternity and his status as the leader of Shiva's attendants.

Ganesha is held in special reverence in Maharashtra, where eight shrines in the vicinity of Pune, collectively called the Ashta Vinayaka, attract huge numbers of worshippers. In a mythological distant past, Ganesha moved over the land, combating evil, spreading good, leaving evidence of his passage in the eight temples, each of which holds part of the sacred spiritual substance, the life force of the deity.

The Ranjangaoncha Mahaganapati temple at Ranjangaon, about 50 kilometres from Pune, enshrines the image of Mahaganapati, who is believed to have here helped Shiva destroy the citadels of the demon Tripurasura. The common myth is presented with a slightly different slant.

> The demon, as many demons do, propitiated Shiva and procured from him a boon of invincibility. Girded by the powers bestowed upon him by the great god, he went on to build three great and completely impregnable citadels, for which he was called Tripurasura. Secure in his strongholds, the demon established his

terrifying and despotic rule over gods and
men. The gods appealed to Shiva for redress
but since he had granted the boon, he was
unable to help. Narada muni heard of
Shiva's dilemma and advised him to
address Mahaganapati, the most powerful
of the gods. Shiva invoked his son with great
humility and implored him to intervene. All
the gods added their pleas and bestowed
their weapons upon Mahaganapati, to aid
him in his destruction of Tripurasura.
Resplendent in his might, utterly confident
and supremely powerful, Mahaganapati
loosened a mighty arrow. It sang through
the air, pierced each of the three
impenetrable citadels of the demon and
killed him instantly. And gods and men
rejoiced.

A variation from South India gives us a
somewhat different version in which Shiva himself
fights the demon.

Moved by the distress of the inhabitants of
the three worlds, Shiva set out to battle the
demon. But he forgot to first seek the

blessings of his son. Insulted, Mahaganapati
caused the axle of Shiva's chariot to break.
As Shiva fell in an undignified heap upon
the ground, he became aware of his
omission. He paid obeisance to his son, who
then empowered his father to vanquish the
demon.

Ganesha as Varadavinayaka, the bestower of
boons, draws thousands of devotees at the
Varadavinayaka temple near Mahad. The shrine
commemorates the legend of Rukmangada.

Once upon a time, King Rukmangada
visited the great sage Vachaknavi. The king
was virtuous and so handsome that the
rishi's wife, Mukundaa, was smitten. She
told the king of her desire. Rukmangada
was horrified and rejected her with anger
and disgust. But Indra, king of the gods,
seized the opportunity. He descended to
earth disguised as Rukmangada and lay
with Mukundaa, to whom a son,
Grutshmada, was born. The boy grew to
manhood, in rectitude and righteousness.
And then one day he discovered his

illegitimacy. Grutshmada was devastated
and grief-stricken at the immorality that
tainted his very being. He prayed to
Ganesha at Bhadrakavana, now called
Mahad, and begged him to absolve the sins
connected with his birth. Moved by his
fervent prayers, Ganesha in his
manifestation as Varadavinayaka granted
his wishes and Grutshmada was liberated
from the sin of his parents.

Thevoor, near Pune, enshrines Ganesha as
Chintamani Vinayaka and is associated with the
familiar myth regarding the dispute over the
possession of the wish-fulfilling gem.

Gana, the son of King Abhijit and Queen
Gunavati, was a great devotee of Shiva.
Pleased with his homage, Shiva granted him
certain powers, which unfortunately went
to Gana's head and inflated his ego.
Once during a visit to sage Kapila's ashram,
Gana saw Kapila's wish-fulfilling gem,
Chintamani, which had been gifted to him
by Shiva. He witnessed its miraculous
powers and felt they were wasted on a mere

sage. Gana believed he would make far
better use of the Chintamani and therefore
deserved to possess the jewel. When Kapila
refused to give it to him, Gana summoned
his army to take the gem by force. But when
he reached Kapila's ashram, he found
Ganesha at the head of a huge army. In the
battle that followed, Gana was killed by
Ganesha who then restored the Chintamani
to Kapila.

The sage returned it to Ganesha. For, he
said, wealth and the desire for riches are
the root of many troubles of the world. He,
however, implored Ganesha to reside at
Thevoor forever, which the devout believe
he indeed does, to this day.

This beautiful temple was often visited by the
Peshwa Madhavarao, who endowed it with immense
riches.

At the Girijaatmaja Vinayaka temple at
Lenayadri, between Pune and Nasik, Ganesha is
revered as an infant.

After Parvati created Ganesha, he grew in
age, prowess and spirituality and came to

be worshipped by mankind. His duties often took him to the far corners of the universe for long periods of time. His mother missed him and grew nostalgic for his childhood. She wistfully recalled with yearning the exploits of his infancy and became seized with longing to see her son as a babe once again. So she meditated and prayed to Ganesha, who, in response, assumed his aspect as the infant Girijaatmaja and came to live in the Lenayadri hills for twelve years. Parvati revelled once again in his childhood and together mother and son performed many miracles.

The Ballaleshwar Vinayak temple at Pali commemorates a legend which describes how Ganapati is said to have come to the aid of a young boy, Ballal.

Long, long ago, a prosperous merchant called Kalyana had a pious young son, Ballal, who was a great devotee of Vinayaka. His fervent devotion inspired other young boys in the neighbourhood, and many of them also dedicated their lives to

worship and prayer. Their fathers were
furious, for they believed that young lads
should work and not spend their days lost
in prayer. They complained to Ballal's
father, who exhorted his son to give up such
foolishness. When Ballal persisted in his
single-minded devotion, Kalyana beat up
the boy and locked him up in a room. But
the lad continued to pray to Ganapati. The
deity appeared before him and, as a reward
for his unwavering devotion, came to live
permanently at Pali, where he was called
Ballal Vinayak.

The powerful image is said to be Swayambhu
(self-generated), and has its trunk turned to the right.
Although this position is considered special and most
rare, the icon of Siddhi Vinayak at the Siddhatek
temple also has the trunk to curving to the right
instead of the more usual orientation towards the
left. The temple is said to be located at the very site
where Ganesha bestowed upon Vishnu the siddhi,
the supra-normal ability, to defeat powerful demons.

Vishnu was in prolonged combat with the
demons Madhu and Kaitabha. Dismayed

at his inability to bring the battle to a
decisive conclusion, he sought the aid of
Shiva who advised him to appeal to
Ganesha. Vishnu did as he suggested. Siddhi
Vinayak appeared on the battlefield, in all
his celestial glory. He blessed Vishnu and
endowed him with the power to vanquish
the demons with ease.

Since that blessed day, say devotees, Siddhi
Vinayaka has granted similar divine powers to
devotees who propitiate the potent image of
Siddhatekcha Vinayaka with the correct rituals. The
temple on top of a hill was constructed by Maharani
Ahilyabai Holkar. Other temples to this aspect of
Ganesha include the famous Siddhi Vinayak temple
in Mumbai, as well as at Pillayarpatti in Tamil
Nadu.

Devotees address Ganesha in many different
ways, through acts of personal prayer and
meditation, through vows and pilgrimages to sacred
sites associated with him. Although Ganesha is
worshipped through the year and in many
circumstances every day, he is specially honoured
on the fourth day of the suklapaksha, the bright half
of the lunar month. The suklapaksha is considered

auspicious for new undertakings while during the krishnapaksha (the dark half) failure is more likely.

The fourth day of the dark half, the samkasta chaturthi, the monthly anniversary of the day Ganesha cursed the moon, is considered particularly ill-omened. When new initiatives on that day are unavoidable, elaborate measures must be performed to avert disaster. These include fasting, feeding twenty-one Brahmins and offering the deity twenty-one of his favourite sweets, modakas. A myth associated with this day describes how Shiva was able to defeat the wicked demon Taraka only because he worshipped Ganesha before going into the battle.

The actual day on which the curse was pronounced was, of course, Ganesha Chaturthi, when it is said that anyone who looks at the moon will be falsely accused of theft or crime. If one were to inadvertently look at the moon, the evil impact, it is believed, can be averted only by throwing stones on a neighbour's roof and being abused in consequence. Another option to ward off the dreadful consequences of viewing the moon is to listen to the story of the Syamantaka jewel, which describes how the blue god, Krishna, himself was mistakenly charged with theft.

Once upon a time, Prince Satrajit obtained
the priceless Syamantaka gem from Surya,
the sun. Krishna offered to keep it safe, but
Satrajit refused and gave it to his brother,
who wore it while hunting and was killed
by a lion. The lion in turn was killed by
Jambavat, king of the bears, who found the
Syamantaka gem and gave it to his son as
a plaything. Meanwhile, when Satrajit's
brother did not return, the prince accused
Krishna of killing him for possession of the
gem. To vindicate himself, Krishna
searched for the jewel and eventually found
it in Jambavat's cave. The bear king
mistook Krishna for an intruder, a second
'false accusation', and fought him till he
suddenly recognized him as the lord.
Jambavat prostrated himself before Krishna
and gladly gave him the jewel and his
daughter Jambavati in marriage. Krishna
then returned the Syamantaka gem to
Satrajit, who was deeply ashamed of his
faithless allegation. He offered to give
Krishna the jewel and his sister Satyabhama
in marriage. Krishna gladly accepted

Satyabhama as his wife but refused to keep
the contentious jewel.

The Ganesha Chaturthi of the month of
Bhadrapada is the focus of special festivities spread
over several days. Images made of unfired clay, to
symbolize Parvati's creation of Ganesha from the
unguents of her body, are installed in homes and
public shrines all over the country. These are
endowed with life through rituals that invoke the
life force (jiva), the breath of being (prana) and the
senses (indriya). Durva grass, on which amrita, the
nectar of immortality, was once spilled is offered to
the image.

The male head of the family, who assumes the
dual role of both host and servant of the lord, wears
red silk, the colour associated with Ganesha and
the purest of cloth. The family then honours Ganesha
by bathing him, but since the clay image would
dissolve if bathed in water, it is substituted with a
betel nut. Treated as an honoured guest, the image
is clothed, given gifts and entertained with songs.
During the one-and-a-half to ten days when
Ganapati resides with the family, prayers are offered
to him in the morning and evening (arti) and hymns
are sung to the accompaniment of small gongs.

Community celebrations, focussed on more elaborate
icons, follow similar patterns in public festivities
called Sarvajanik Ganeshotsava.

Group worship of Ganesha originated in
Maharashtra in the late nineteenth century, when
Lokamanya Bal Gangadhar Tilak fostered such
celebrations as an innovative tool in the struggle
for the political liberation of India. He used this
festival to bring together various Hindu sects and to
bridge the chasm between Brahmins and lower caste
Hindus. Subscriptions were collected for the
installation of large images in gaily decorated
community pavilions. These became the focus of
public worship where patriotic songs implored
Ganesha's aid in obtaining freedom. The militant
flavour was often accentuated by costumed
attendants in the garb of Shivaji's soldiers, who
demonstrated their prowess in various traditional
martial arts performed during the festivities. When
Tilak died in 1920, the Ganesha festival petered
out, only to be revived with great enthusiasm in
later years, when it also spread to other parts of the
country.

Both family and community images are taken
for immersion in a procession on the day of Ganesha
Chaturthi itself. Before leaving, the house holder or

patron symbolically closes the eyes of the image
with sprigs of durva grass dipped in honey, thus
dispersing the vital breath. The entire family, or
community, accompanies the image to the water
body chosen for immersion. Processions are
accompanied by singing and dancing, through clouds
of vermilion powder flung into the air by devotees.
The rite of immersion, Ganesha visarjan, is
concluded at the edge of the water. Final gifts of
coconuts, flowers and lighted camphor are offered
to images while hymns call upon Ganesha to return
early next year:

> O, Ganesha, lord of Moriya,
> please return soon next year.
> We are sad that you have departed,
> for your presence brings us peace.

Images, once immersed, quickly dissolve,
recalling the cosmic cycle of formlessness giving
way to form and then moving again towards
formlessness. Mantras emphasizing Ganesha's
omniscience and omnipotence are chanted as the
images are washed away. His 108 names are
invoked, and the devotee concludes:

Thou art my father and my mother,
Thou art my relative and friend,
Thou art my wisdom and my wealth,
Thou art my everything, o god of gods.

For his followers, Ganesha provides an anchor in a confusing, ever-changing world. He is the accessible god, compassionate and easy to please, who satisfies every human need, be it spiritual, emotional or material.

The many myths and legends about Ganesha have inspired and comforted countless millions and offered clues to the meaning and purpose of life. They are as relevant today as they ever were. It is for us to draw upon the stories and make innovations in our own lives, to renew the art of joy and love, to conquer our own demons, to see that obstacles are often self-created. Only then will Ganesha endure, releasing his life-sustaining power for all eternity.